From The CELL To The CROSS

Dennis Page

Printed in the U.S.A.

Cover design by Penny Hall
Text design by Greg Solie – Altamont Graphics

ISBN 10 0-9789718-0-9
ISBN 13 978-0-9789718-0-9

—Contents—

—Dedication—

This book is gratefully dedicated to the following:

To Jesus Christ, the Lamb of God, for loving me and revealing Himself to me at a time in my life when I thought it was about to end; and for showing me an example by which I am to live my life. For His blood that cleanses me from my sins; for His intercession on my behalf and much more.

To God the Father, for giving His only Son to redeem us from the snares of Satan; a gift of love that will be spoken of for all eternity. I will praise Thee in the midst of the congregation and will share my testimony with all and forever praise Thy name.

—Acknowledgments—

With loving acknowledgements:

To my son, Travis, who has loved me unconditionally and has encouraged me in trying times. I thank him for his patience and sharing me with others that they too may come to know Jesus Christ. Thank you, my son, for your love, compassion and being supportive of the ministry the Lord has called me to. May God manifest Himself to you in a greater way than He has made Himself known to me.

To my son's mother, Lori, who was there for me when nobody else was and always made sure that I could stay in contact with my son, and in her own way ministering to me while I was incarcerated. Thank you for showing me compassion. May God open your eyes that you may behold His Son Jesus Christ in a way that you have never seen Him before, that your life may be greatly enriched.

To my brothers and sisters in Christ Jesus who ministered to me when I was in prison out of their Bible School, sending me the *Amazing Facts* Bible Studies and words of encouragement. May God richly bless this ministry.

To all those at 3ABN who made it possible for me to share my testimony around the world. Thank you and may God bless this ministry and those who watch 3ABN with an outpouring of His Holy Spirit.

I also praise God and give thanks to Him for raising up Remnant Publications to be a tool in His hands in spreading the Gospel in various ways. I thank Dawn Caros for the editing she has done and Penny Hall for the art work on the cover. I also want to thank Judy Jennings for the advice and direction she offered. I pray that God's blessing and grace will be upon all the workers of Remnant for their help.

—Introduction—

I have written this book after being inspired by God to do so. It is a short story of my life growing up in search of love and acceptance. I have never done anything with my life except cause pain to others as well as myself. I never thought that there was hope for me after living a life consumed with alcohol, drugs, and immoral living.

My friend, if you are currently living a life of pain and misery, a life that you believe has no other hope, please read this book, and may you receive a blessing as you read this testimony of my life and my experience with Jesus Christ. My desire is for those that have traveled down the same pathway of crime and wretchedness to know that hope can be found in the name of Jesus Christ, the Son of the Living God.

Jesus is waiting for all that will call upon Him for help. I can testify to the fact that it is scary to travel down an unfamiliar road. You see, I knew that to continue my chaotic life of drugs and corruption would, in the end, only lead to death. Sadly, because I was familiar with this environment, I was willing to accept this future. There are so many people in the world today that feel comfortable living abusive, corrupt, and destructive lifestyles that they are afraid to venture down a different path, even if it means a better life. They know what to expect in the lifestyle in which they are currently living, and to travel down a new path is frightening. I know it certainly was for me.

It is now my desire to reach these people by sharing the love Jesus Christ has shown me as He has lifted me up out of a life of misery, healing my broken heart and leading me down a new road of peace. A few passages from the book of *Psalms* sums it up:

"He brought me up also out of an horrible pit, out of the miry clay, and set my feet upon a rock, [and] established my goings." Psalms 40:2

"He (God) will regard the prayer of the destitute, and not despise their prayer. This shall be written for the generation to come: and the people which shall be created shall praise the Lord. For He hath looked down from the height of His sanctuary; from heaven did the LORD behold the earth. To hear the groaning of the prisoner; to loose those that are appointed to death." Psalms 102:17–20

May your faith be increased as you read how God heard my cry and reached out to help me.

—One—
My Beginning

From the few conversations that my mother has been willing to have with me concerning her past, I have been able to gather a little background of her life. She was given the name, Patricia Deitz, and raised in Buffalo, New York. Raised in a physically and mentally abusive family, her mother was an alcoholic and a very short tempered woman. I don't know anything about her father, since she has never spoken of him.

At an early age my mother rebelled and got pregnant when she was only 13 years old. She didn't know what to do, scared and confused she entered a Catholic convent. Here they helped her through her pregnancy and found someone to adopt the son she gave birth to. He would now be about 51 years of age. When she was 18 she left the convent and was looking for a way to get out of the city.

One of her girlfriends was dating a man by the name of Dennis Earl Smith. He was serving in the US Navy on an aircraft carrier called the *USS Exess*. Apparently this couple broke up and my mother started dating Dennis. They moved to Rhode Island, for his ship was docked in the harbor in that area. Shortly after, my mother secured false identification, under the name of Patricia Deitzwitch, which showed her to be old enough to wed without parental permission. In 1962, Dennis and my mother were married in Quontset Point, Rhode Island.

Not long after their marriage, they moved to Cheektowaga, New York, Dennis's home town. Within the year, the Smith couple became a happy family when I was born. My parents named me Dennis, after my father, and were thrilled with their new baby boy. I was still an infant when my mother became pregnant with my sister, Daneen, soon nicknamed Gidget, after the 60s TV show.

Perhaps the quick growth of the family was too much stress, or there were other troubles in their young marriage, but shortly thereafter my parents separated. My mother kept no information or pictures to show me. Only recently has she shared the basic circumstances of my birth, in fact, imagination has filled in the possible happenstance of their actual meeting. It is my prayer that one day I might meet my father.

—Two—
Growing Up

Some early childhood memories are strongly imprinted in my mind. I believe my sister and I were five and six years old, when we woke up early one morning and decided that we did not like the way the new kitchen chairs looked with the vinyl lining around the upper part of the chair. So, we found some sharp knives and began to cut the vinyl lining off the chair. We also lit some matches and dropped them on the table. My mother was furious when she caught us and the punishment was one I will never forget. She turned on the burner of the stove and dragged us over to the flame, one at a time, putting our hands just close enough to feel the intense heat. We were terrified that day!

Shortly after that, in the middle of the winter in Buffalo, New York, we tried to run away to grandmother's house. Mom had left for work and we were to get on the bus and go to school. Instead, we began to pack up what we would need for the trip. We filled brown paper bags with some blankets and some canned goods. We thought, if we had to, we could camp out and have a snack as well. We could only remember the way the city bus ran and tried to follow that route. I remember the big, white, fluffy snow flakes falling all around us that day and that the chill of the air soon began to sink in our bones. I recall walking under an overpass and thinking of camping for a short time. Looking at my sister, I could see that she was freezing. Our brown paper bags were getting wet from the snow and were beginning to tear. We decided to head back home.

When we arrived at home my mother was there to greet us at the door. As we approached the door it opened, and there was mom holding a can opener in her hand. She said,

"Did you forget something?" We went on in and got warm. It was very quiet in our home that day. I don't recall much else, but perhaps my mother was really thinking about the way things were in our home.

At the age of seven my mother remarried and I remember that day clearly because of something my mother said to me. I had been looking through what I remember to be a Children's Bible at my grandmother's house. I don't know what inspired my mother to say this, but she told me that God was going to destroy the world in the year 2000. (Perhaps this was what my mother was taught in the Catholic convent as a child). Soon after that I figured out how old I would be when I would die due to this destruction. I would be 37 years of age. As a child I put this in the back of my mind. The year 2000 seemed a very long way off, but it was an experience I never forgot!

When I was 8 my mother gave birth to a boy, who she named George Washington Page, after his father. My sister and I often helped out with my little brother, feeding and changing diapers as well as playing with him. I also spent a lot of time by myself building models and playing with my race-track that my grandmother bought me.

When I was 11 years old, my parents let my sister and me spend the night at a friend of theirs where they would often go to play cards and drink. It was not the first time that we stayed there, but this time the oldest boy molested me that night. I never told anyone and it has been very hard for me to talk about it even to this day. My sister was attacked and thrown into a dumpster about one year later down the street from our house. The sad part about this was that people watched it happen, but no one helped her until after it was done.

At the age of 12, my mother gave me my first drink; it was a shot of tequila. By the time I was 13, my stepfather taught me how to gamble, and I started picking up his pornographic magazines and reading them. My childhood was doomed from the beginning. So many parents fail to realize that their behavior and the things they partake of have a great influence on their children. Parents set the stage for their children's character early in life.

We did not grow up in a Christian atmosphere, and I had only been to church a few times with my grandparents. My parents did their own thing and left my siblings and me to figure out life on our own. Our parents told us not to do this and that; to be polite and not to steal, kind of a basic outline on how to be good. We were to do as they said and not as they did. Well, of course, as a child this raises a lot of questions as to why do you do these things and we can't? This is where my rebellion started, fueled by the though of "when I get older I can do as I please!"

As a child I was not taught the principle of "love because you care," it was more of a "love" out of fear. We were to do as we were told or face the consequences of punishment. After becoming calloused to the stern hand that was placed upon me for disobedience, I began to rebel more. Consequently, I learned to endure other unusual punishments that were placed upon me, such as being forced to kneel down with my arms stretched out to the sides and if they were to drop, the next thing I might feel is the belt swatting me across my backside. I might be made to lean against the wall on my finger tips, or sent to my room to endure solitude. Instead of being taught to do the right things out of love with the parents setting the example, we learned to obey out of fear of physical punishment. Fortunately, through God's leading, I learned to discipline my own son with love according to God's Word.

(I would like to add—to this day I love my mother and truly have forgiven her. You see, she could only raise me with the tools in which she was given in life. She could only treat me in the same way in which she herself had been taught. This is how the chain of abuse continues).

There always seemed to be a lot of fighting going on between my mother and stepfather, so I did not understand the concept of love. As a child I was, in my own little way, searching for love and acceptance. Because I did not feel it at home, I looked for it in the friends that I made in the streets. It was there that I started to figure out the concept of every man for himself, or in my case, every child for himself. I had only a couple of friends that I would hang out with and we would often just walk the streets thinking of ways to cause mischief.

At the age of 14, my parents decided to move to a small town in Indiana because the company my dad had been working for moved to Canada. I was finishing up the 8th grade and was not at all interested in changing schools or meeting new kids. I pretty much kept to myself during the remainder of the school year. I was bored because what they were teaching I had already been taught in the 6th grade. I could not figure out why they were so far behind. On the other hand, this was neat because I didn't have to do any studying for about 2 years.

I made my first real friend in 9th grade; his name was Jeff K. He came up to me, introduced himself and invited me over. I was a shy kid and probably would have kept to myself for quite some time before trying to make friends. The first thing I noticed about my new friend's family was that his parents weren't around much either. I wanted to fit in, so I started to drink and do drugs with the rest of the kids; from the time I was a young child I just wanted to be accepted and tried to understand what one would have to do to accomplish this.

Often my stepfather would threaten me, saying that he was going to send me to some type of military school for obedience training. At the age of 16, near the end of my junior year, I talked with a Marine Corp recruiter to see what it would take for me to join the Marines. He told me that if my parents would sign a waiver, I could start going to reserve meetings during my senior year, and after my graduation I could go to boot camp. So, I made up my mind to do this. I wanted to prove to my parents that I had no problem with discipline, but that my problem was just trying to understand them. With their approval, I completed my boot camp training and then trained for combat engineer. I came back home, attended reserve meetings, and started a full time job.

—THREE—
Still in Search of Love and Acceptance

After returning home from the Marines I was looking forward to getting my own place; but to my surprise, the money that I had sent home to be put away for me had been spent. I did not understand what the problem was, but it did not take long to figure out; my step dad was, and still is, a compulsive gambler.

As with all addictions, people don't care about anything else but self and how to feed their addiction. Often this is achieved by taking advantage of someone else. Addicts are never able to see the effect it has on the lives of those around them because they are too busy chasing the rush or feeling from their first experience. A street term we would use is "chasing the dragon." This term is appropriate to use as one continues to chase after the feeling of self-exaltation, pride, or pleasure seeking, wanting to fill the passions of the flesh; it is all evil and in reality one is just chasing the Dragon—Satan. All of these self-seeking things will only end in destruction. I myself fell prey to these evils, but mine were through the intimidation I learned from my mother, and drugs.

In my search for acceptance, I thought that if I had something to offer people they would not only be my friend, but would accept me. You see, I thought acceptance meant love, which I so desperately needed; so I started selling drugs. I knew a lot of people that partied and I figured that I could give them a product they wanted at a fair price. I always had a good job to support myself, but did this on the side. I began selling marijuana, but soon started selling cocaine as well.

I got married when I was 25 to a woman that I had been with for about 3 years. It did not last long because of my lifestyle, which she knew about, but perhaps she thought she could change me. Here I was too blinded by my addiction of cocaine use to understand her concern for my health and her love for me. She was the first person in my life that did love me for myself and not for what I could offer her. She perhaps could see something inside of me that I could not. To this day, I am deeply sorry for the pain that I caused her. This, too, is a prayer of mine that she forgives me.

Within a few months I met Lori. Again a relationship started for all the wrong reasons. I still did not understand the difference between acceptance and love. My whole life I misunderstood the difference between the two. Just because someone accepted me surely did not mean they loved me.

When I was 30, Lori gave birth to our son. We name him Travis Wade Page. I loved my son very much, and it sure was neat watching him grow up. The sad part was that I still did not change my lifestyle as a drug dealer and user. Once again; because of this, Lori and I split up and went our separate ways.

Today, I thank God that Lori realized it was best for Travis to be involved in my life. Little did she know he was the one thing that kept me somewhat accountable for my behavior and responsibility as a father.

My son has always shown me pure and honest love. He liked to help with whatever I was doing in the kitchen or any remodeling work around the house. He also liked to help outside, too. He was, and still is, a big animal lover. We had a beautiful German shepherd named Caesar. It broke both of our hearts the day he died. He had started losing weight, and one evening he would not eat at all, so I took him to the vet. They did a blood test and called me later that evening to tell me that he had some disease and that I should bring him back in the morning when they would get him started on some medication. Unfortunately, he did not make it. He died that night in my son's bedroom. The vet told me that he thought there was something else wrong because he had not seen an animal die that fast from that disease.

Today, as my son and I remember our pet Caesar, we think about the time when God will recreate the world. We look forward to playing with all the animals that will be there in the new earth. It is here that we hope to see our pet and friend Caesar again.

—Four—
Invited to Go to Church

At the age of 35, I was invited to go to church by my employer. It kind of caught me off guard. You see, he knew that I used and sold drugs. I had a reputation and I did not care if people knew. I was a good worker, and that is all most employers care about; but this man and his wife were different. God was reaching out to me but I did not understand. Danny and Evett are very kind, caring people. When he asked, my answer was, "No." You see, I believed that my fate was sealed because of the choices I made in life, the things I had done and was still doing. Then, he asked if they could take my son to church and I said, "Yes." I told him that if I was ever going to do anything right with my life it was to make sure my son knew who Jesus Christ is. I thought that if he could know Jesus before all the corruption of the world crept in, he would have a better chance than I did; for myself, I thought there was no hope, but for him, there was hope. Danny and Evett took my son to church a couple of times, and he really enjoyed himself.

Perhaps here God was working to draw me to Him through my son, but I was too entangled in darkness to fully see or understand. It is my hope to speak with this couple again some day to thank them for their acts of kindness and prayers. I also did them a great injustice in the way I left their company and would like the opportunity to ask them for their forgiveness.

Shortly after this, a co-worker, Dave, invited my son and me to go to church with his family. I decided to give it a chance. I believe I went to church with Dave and his wife Sheila, about 3 or 4 times. I don't remember what the sermons or studies were about, but my son seemed to enjoy himself. After a few times I stopped going; I just did not feel right going to church. I was an evil person; and after all, I thought there was no hope for people like me.

—Five—
Taking Up a New Drug

Over the next couple of years, I started dealing with some different people out of Mexico. I switched from cocaine to methamphetamine. I was burnt out on cocaine after 17 years of use. I started smoking and selling meth as it was becoming a very popular drug in high demand.

From time to time I would rent out one of the extra bedrooms in my house in order to help with the bills. This time I rented to one of the Mexican guys I was buying from; I'll call him Sergio. During this time I started to meet some of his friends and once in a while I would see the person he was picking up from. He would come over and make a drop, but not in front of me; they would do business in another room.

After a while things were not going too well. I was in need of product and Sergio would just hold out on delivery. I knew he had it, but I did not understand what his problem was. I had established a steady flow of business, and I did not want to lose my customers to another supplier; so one time, when the "big guy" called, I asked if I could speak with him sometime and he agreed.

I had earned a good report with the people higher up in the organization once by exposing someone in their circle that was ripping them off and when they could not find this person, I did. This person had made the mistake of coming over, not knowing that I was now doing business with these people. I looked upon this as an opportunity to establish a better relationship. I made a phone call and delayed him there until they came. I even told them they could "off him" there if they wanted to, but they just took him for a ride.

Another time I brought it to their attention that one of the people they were doing a little business with was working undercover for the drug task force. From that point on I started doing some of my business directly from the main guy and sometimes from Sergio. For some reason they did not want Sergio to know that I was dealing direct.

One day I asked Sergio to move out, so he got his own place. Shortly after this I was listening to messages on my answering machine. At the end of the messages I found a partial recording of a conversation with Sergio and the boss man. I heard the boss man tell Sergio to shut off the machine, but he did not do it. I then found out that one of the friends of Sergio, (I'll call him Juan) was lying about the amount of time he had been in this country. I had asked the boss man once how long he knew Sergio and Juan and how long they had been in the country. He told me that they had been here for five years.

Later, I happened to be doing some business in a different town and talked with someone who mentioned Juan's name. His real name was not a very common one, so I asked for a description of the person, and it was the same person I knew. I asked my friend how long she had known him. Her husband said his best friend had gone to school with him. Well, my jaw just about hit the floor. Now, it was all starting to come together.

I took the answering machine tape and this other information to the boss man. At first he did not believe it, but I told him that I had a person who could prove that Juan had been in this country for at least 15 years. It was clear to me that either the FBI or the DEA had an agent worked in.

—Six—
Picking Up on Surveillance

I realized it was time to pick up a scanner. I had a friend program it for the local task force, FBI, and DEA. He also got me hooked up with the undercover channel called Ileen, which the local task force would switch over to from time to time when doing surveillance. It was also programmed to pick up wireless mics and bugs. I also had a device that could hook up to my phone to let me know if it was tapped or if my conversation was being recorded.

It was not long before I picked up on the task force setting up surveillance on my home and tapping my phone. This did not bother me. I kept on dealing, figuring I was always one step ahead of them. After about 6 months I knew that they wanted our whole group, not just me. So I made a game out of it.

Meanwhile, the boss man was starting to get a little concerned with this new information about Sergio and Juan. He set up a meeting with me and the guys above him. At this meeting we talked about these issues, and then went our separate ways.

A short time later I was having lunch with the boss man at a restaurant that belonged to a friend of his. During lunch, he excused himself saying that he had to go outside to talk to someone. Soon after he left, in came a Mexican guy walking very slowly up to my table with his hands in his jacket pockets. As he was approaching, he was looking around the room to see if anybody was watching our table. I knew this was not good, but I figured I was in a public place so I was not too worried. This man walked up to my table, turned his back to me, looked around the room, then sat down in the chair right across from me and just watched the people to see if anyone was watching us. He never looked at me and I just kept eating my lunch. He then got up and left. The boss man came back in and sat down. There was no need for me to ask what was going on; I could put two and two together, although I was not completely sure.

A couple of days later, the phone rang and the boss man wanted to stop by to pick up some money. I told him to come on over and to use his key. (I had given him a key to my house so he could check things out at any time. I wanted him to know that I had nothing to hide, because it was shortly after I had given him information about Sergio and Juan that Sergio started saying that I was the one working for the Feds.) When he arrived I happened to be in the kitchen, and I greeted him at the door. As I was shutting the door, I noticed that the guy sitting in the car was the same one as in the restaurant. I knew then, for sure, what was going on. I confronted the boss man about this and he denied it. I was not stupid; dealing with these people I knew that if they were unsure about who was telling the truth they would just eliminate us both. Sad to say, to me it was still a big game. I never valued my life for I had never really been valued by anyone.

Reader, if you feel that your life has no value, I would like you to think on this. If you were the only sinner in the whole world, God would have still sent His only Son into the world to die to redeem you. When you think that your life has no value, know that God the Father has placed a great value upon your life for He gave His only Son to die on the cross to redeem you back to Him.

—SEVEN—
Talking with the Dead

One night a friend of mine was house-sitting down the street and asked me to come over. I'll call her Jill. I had known her for about 17 years and we had previously dated for awhile. I really liked her a lot and we remained friends although the relationship did not work out. So I went down and we partied together for awhile. Then she said that she wanted to talk to me about something. She asked me not to tell anyone, and then proceeded to explain that ever since she was a little girl, she had been having conversations with spirits. She believed these to be people that had died. She then told me that one of them wanted to talk with me and began to give me a description of the spirit. She seemed to be in some type of a trance as I think back. The spirit that she described I believed to be my grandmother who had passed away some years back. I never talked to my friend about my grandmother and she had never seen a picture of her. So I truly believed it was my grandmother. She told me that there were a couple of other spirits there too, and one of them was just standing there with arms folded, but no description was given. She said that my grandmother was saying that I needed to spend more time with my son and to help the other children. There were some other things, but I was so shocked that I don't remember them. I understood the part about my son because I was really caught up in the drug game and was slacking as a father. I did not understand about the other children until later.

A couple of days went by and some strange things started happening around my house. I would crash out and wake up to books being moved around. A couple of times my stereo would just come on or shut off for no apparent reason. It seemed as if someone, who was not there, was trying to talk to me. When I asked Jill about it she told me that the spirits wanted to talk to me. Of course I asked, "Why?" She said it was because I would listen to them.

One evening I was getting something out of my car at Jill's house, and as I opened the passenger side door a dark shadow rose up over the back of the car and looked at me. It scared me half to death. Then it was gone. I never told my friend; I just went home after all of that.

Reader, with the elevating rate of spiritualism in the world it is very important that we understand what we are truly dealing with. (Please see page 122 for Biblical information regarding the state of the dead. Are the dead really dead? And who are these modern psychics talking to?)

Now, another friend of mine, (I'll call her Kelly) came by one day very upset. She started telling me about some people that were involved in child pornography. One of them happened to be her boyfriend. As she continued to look into things she found out that some of his friends were involved as well. These people happened to be police officers. This did not surprise me. I knew some of the officers were corrupt. I had done cocaine with one of them who used to do moonlighting at a club I would go to occasionally. One of the head detectives used my friend Kelly to sleep with her. She was one of those kinds of girls. This same detective was told a year before this started to go down that I had him on video engaging in unlawful activity. My friend Kelly told me that he was very eager to get his hands on these videos. Of course I told her that they were in a safe place and would only be used if necessary.

She would work both sides, so that if she got in trouble with the law she had a way out. I was also aware of some of the officers giving the drugs they would confiscate to Narcs to feed their habits as well as allowing them to use this as a means of entrapment. Now, I understood about the children.

—EIGHT—
Almost Killed by the Police

One night I was sitting at home when I got a phone call from someone who began to threaten to come over and do me some harm. (Of course he used different language). His ex-girlfriend had been buying from me and he did not like it. I told him to come on over, that I had something for him. Meanwhile, I had to shovel some snow off my roof. We had quite a bit, and the ice was backing up under my shingles causing water to leak in the house. I figured I would go up to do that and at the same time see what the surveillance team was up to. By now I had pretty much figured out a couple of the vehicles. I also thought I should take a weapon out with me in case the caller stopped by.

All I had on me was a couple of rifles at that time; I had just sold the only handgun I had. I took the 9mm rifle out with me. I always carried my scanner around so I could listen to what the police were doing. I went out back, set up a ladder, and then came back in to lock the sliding glass doors which could only be locked from the inside. As soon as I walked out front and turned to lock my front door, I heard a report come over the scanner, "Subject has a weapon." I looked around, but I thought I was just being paranoid. I said to myself, "They can't be talking about me." Then, as I was walking around back I heard them say, "Subject is going around back." Then I knew! A few days earlier I thought I had seen a couple of officers in my neighbor's house across the street, but I was not sure. They had their blinds pulled down part way and all I could see was the lower part of some uniforms. They had a big bay window in the front of their house and never in the 6 years I had been living there had they ever shut the blinds.

Now I knew the police had set up across the street. This did not really bother me. I lived in the country, and had the right to have firearms.

I proceeded around back and up the ladder; I got up on the roof and just stood there for a couple of moments listening for what they might say next. I had started to shovel snow off the roof when I heard. "Dispatch, this is squad two requesting permission to pull out. Subject is on the roof with weapon." I stopped shoveling and just watched. I could see the neighborhood pretty well from my roof. A blazer came around from the street behind my house; two snowmobiles and a van came from down the street. They all met behind some woods just down the street across from the front of my house. I just stared, listening for their next move. Then it came, "Dispatch, squad two requesting permission to jump the gun." I knew then I was in big trouble! They were requesting to come over and take me out! They thought I was going to use my firearm to engage them in a conflict.

I used to have a laser on the end of a pen, and from time to time I would mess with them by pointing it out the window in their direction. They finally had enough!

I did not hesitate. I left the rifle on the roof, went into the house and called my mother. Yes, my mother. I've always been open with my mother as to what I was doing. She did not like it, but I was her son and she did, in her own way, love me. I knew my phone was tapped so I figured that if I repeated that reason why I had the weapon in the first place, they might get it this time.

This is how the conversation went:

"Hello, Mom."

"How are you doing son?"

"Not good, look, I want to let you know what is going on over here. As you know, I told you that the task force has been watching me and that they have tapped my phone. Now earlier, a person called me and was making some threats and said that he was going to come over, so I told him, 'fine.' Meanwhile, I had to shovel some snow off my roof so I went up to do that. I figured I would take a weapon up with me in case this person came by. My intentions were to just scare him off by shooting a few rounds into the yard. I know my phone is being tapped; and you know these guys hear my phone conversations but they don't listen."

"What do you mean?"

"Well, when I went up on the roof they pulled back their surveillance team because they thought I went up on the roof to take shots at them. Now they are requesting permission to come over and take me out. I just want to let you know in case something does go down. I'll call you back later OK?"

"Alright, but be careful!"

I went back up on the roof to watch for their next move. Within minutes the answer came over the scanner. "Squad two, this is dispatch. That is a negative on 'jump the gun,' subject has weapon for trespasser only." I watched as they slowly drove off. I finished shoveling off the roof and went inside.

Being the antagonist that I was, over the next couple of days I started to call up my friends to make fun of the officers because they were running like a bunch of scared rabbits; but all I did was add more gas to the fire. Here God saved my life again, and I did not even know it.

Reader, I would like you to take a moment and reflect back on your life. Think about how many times God has stepped in and saved your life. If you can only think of a few times, you're wrong. You see, Satan is trying to destroy you every day, and it is by the mercy of God that you are alive right now. Every one of you reading this book owes your life to God, as does every person alive. If one could have their eyes opened to see the spiritual battle taking place around them, they would truly run to the Lord and hang onto Him as if their very life depended upon it; for it truly does!

—NINE—
God Reveals Himself to Me

A couple of weeks passed and I was really getting tired, I knew it was just a matter of time and either I'd wind up dying from doing too much dope or one of two groups would wind up killing me. I did not care anymore. For the last 6 or 8 months I had been writing out my feelings, and many times I would just cry from loneliness. I had a very nice home with everything in it, an in ground pool, nice car, and money was not a problem; but I felt so empty inside. I was angry with my parents for the way they raised me. I felt rejected my whole life by them. When I joined the Marines I thought they would be proud of me, but instead they just took advantage of the money I sent home.

I've had my heart broken many times. I would fall in love very easily. If a woman showed affection towards me I would just hang on. I hungered to be loved, but it always turned to hurt. The inner pain in my life was too much. I finally reached the end and did not care if I lived or died. At about 2:00 a.m. one morning, I started to write; but this time, for some unexplained reason, I started with the word "Jesus." This is what came out:

As Words Flow Through Me to You

Jesus said: For I told you I would never be far away as I feel and hear your hearts cry out today.

The People say: What must we do? Where should we pray? And where is it safe for our children to play. With all the evil in the world today, our Saviour, can you say?

Jesus says: The answers have been placed in your hearts from the very start. True faith will see you through.

The People say: With all the evil in the world today, it is our faith we are to rely on?

Jesus says: Yes, for the end days have now come. I will test the faith in everyone.

I say: Have no fear for Jesus is here. Do you not feel Him? Is it not clear? His Spirit is everywhere. Put all you trust and faith in the Father and the Son, and They will guide you and protect you from the wicked one. And I also would like people to live their lives with this in mind. Treat the person next to you as if that person was Jesus Christ and then and only then would the world be a better place for me and you and our families.

I put this aside without reading it and started to write another paper. All of a sudden, I heard loud footsteps running down my hallway upstairs. This gave me a pretty good scare. I knew that what was up there was not human. There had been spirit activity going on around my house. There was no need for me to go upstairs, I was sure no one was in my house. I went back to writing and from the corner of my eye caught a glimpse of a silhouette of what I thought was a person across the room; for some strange reason, I was not afraid. I went back to writing. The figure walked right past me and sat down beside me. I just kept writing; I wanted to look but I could not. It was as if my head was locked in place. When I was done writing the second paper, I picked up the first paper and read it.

For the first time in my life I felt peace. I'll never forget that feeling. I now knew God was real. I had heard people say things before and I had <u>thought</u> I believed though I was not really sure; but <u>now</u> I was sure! I remember dancing around the room with joy as this was the first time in my life I felt true peace and hope. Whenever I hear the song "Amazing Grace," I always think of this night, for truly God's grace is amazing!

Reader, do you remember the first time that grace appeared to you? If not, try to think back and embrace that moment every time you come into trials or you feel overwhelmed by the circumstances around you. For God has never left you; He is still there. Just continue to call upon the name of Jesus Christ. I once read:

> *"The only thing we have to fear in the future is to forget how God has led us in the past." The Pilgrim's Progress, John Bunyan*

—Ten—
First Time Witnessing

By now it was about 2:45 a.m., and I had to share what just happened with someone. I called up some people that I knew would be up and asked if I could come over; they said, "Yes." I went over and shared with them what had happened and read the poem to them. They were shocked, I don't quite remember our whole conversation but they probably thought that I had really gone over the edge. I probably would have thought the same thing if things were reversed. After all, I never talked about Jesus Christ or the Bible; to them I was their drug dealer, nothing more.

On the way home I started to recall all the events that led up to that night. I did not understand what God wanted with me. I began crying, and I asked God, "What do You want with me? Can't you see the type of person I am?" I realized God was for real and I was scared. I now started thinking that perhaps He was going to put me down because of all my evil doings.

The next day I continued to share my experience with the people I was selling drugs to. I also was sharing with the main guy that I was buying from. Everybody thought I was going off the deep end. I don't think they believed me; however, when I shared the poem, I think it had a few of them wondering what was really happening.

Witnessing is now one of my favorite things to do. I get really excited when talking to others about Jesus, especially the way He saved me and how He continues to teach and provide for me daily. I do believe that anyone who truly realizes what Christ has done for them on a personal level will not be able to keep it in; and as they grow in the grace and knowledge of Jesus Christ they will continue to share. For they will feel as if they are going to burst if they don't share the light and grace they receive from Christ.

It saddens my heart knowing what Jesus is doing in a person's life and they act as if it is no big deal, such as contributing a blessing from God to just luck or good fortune. Sadly, there is just a small few who truly acknowledge God, our Father, as the One who sustains our lives. What joy so many miss out on by not witnessing for Jesus Christ and praising Him for what He is doing in their lives.

—Eleven—
First Time Reading the Bible

After I got home that night I got out a Bible that Dave and Sheila gave to me after going to church with them a few times, just before all of this happened. I just opened it up and started to read. I opened it up to the Gospels. I don't remember which one, but I do remember as I started to read, it was as if God was talking right to me. I was so overwhelmed with everything that I began to cry. I was scared, I did not understand, and I felt so alone, but I did not give up. I wanted to know if there was anything in the Bible that had to do with me.

Reader, if you have started to read the Bible and stopped because it was not making any sense to you, I encourage you to please begin again. Keep this in mind, when a child first hears a parent speaking to them they don't understand. As that child continues to hear they begin to understand a little at a time. We are God's children, and when we first begin to read His Word it may not make any sense; but, I assure you that if you ask Him to send the Holy Spirit to help you understand, He will. The Bible says:

> *"Ask, and it shall be given you; seek, and ye shall find; knock, and it shall be opened unto you." Matthew 7:7*

God is very loving and He longs to speak to you to bring you comfort and guidance.

So I began my search, but not without problems. First of all, I knew that the task force that was watching me would just as soon kill me then arrest me. I also knew it was just a matter of time before the drug ring I was involved in would make the decision to eliminate me. In addition, I had this major drug addiction that I could not stop. All I could see was darkness, with the exception of the light that had just flashed before me in this experience with God. Oh, what a dark pit I was in! Looking up, all I could see was a raindrop of light that splashed upon my heart. With all odds against me, including my self-destructive lifestyle, if God was going to save me He truly would have to perform not just one miracle, but several.

—Twelve—
Time to Make a Change

After all this I knew it was time to make a change, but I really did not know where to begin. My life was so out of control. Knowing that some of the officers were just as corrupt as me, I figured I should contact someone about them and pass on some of the information that I had come across so that perhaps an investigation would be started on them. This seemed kind of crazy, but I was running out of time and feeling desperate.

I sat down with the man I had been getting my drugs from and again explained to him about my experience with God. I had already informed him that we were being watched. He was always being updated with all the activities as they took place. Of course, he was shocked. I really don't know what was going through his mind, but again I had to witness. I could not keep this experience inside! I then told him my plan to contact a Secret Service agent and give him this information about the officers. I had also talked to my friend Kelly about all of this as well. While she was living with an accountant, she had gained possession of a lot of documents with records of their money flow.

The boss was not happy to hear this, but he trusted me enough to keep on supplying me with drugs. He probably figured he would use me as long as possible then kill me. (At this point in my life, I became pretty bold. I remember telling him one time that if he killed me, he and his whole family would pay a great consequence.)

I made contact with the Secret Service in Washington and asked to speak to an agent, requesting that he not approach me with any local authorities. I explained that I had some information for them concerning some of the local police in that area that were involved in things they would be interested in. Money laundering was one of them. To be sure that they would send someone soon, I added that I thought that there might be an assassination attempt on the President, and that I was concerned about them using any of these officers in setting up security for him when he came. You see, the President was coming to a college near me to give a speech. So, being as crafty as I could be to accomplish what I wanted, I took advantage of the events that were about to take place around me. I told the agent that I was talking with that if he thought I was joking to do a military background check on me. I then gave him my Social Security number. My thoughts on this were that if they would check my file they would not find out much.

The reason for this was when I came back from boot camp and my schooling for combat engineering, I reported to my reserve base and was supposed to turn in my original orders, medical, and dental records to my Commanding Officer. Well, I forgot to do so, and they forgot to ask. So I just put them in my locker and that is where they stayed until I left, and then I took them home with me. As far as I could tell if somebody was to pull up my military records to check me out they would not find out too much about me. My goal was to lead them to think that I did more for the government than what appeared.

About a week later a Secret Service agent called and made arrangements to come over. I'll call him John. When John showed up he had another person with him. John introduced himself, showed me his ID, and then introduced the person with him, who happened to be a detective on the force at the very same police department that I had planned to give information about.

When Agent John introduced the other man, I told him, "Yes, I know who he is." The look on the agent's face said it all. I knew that the heat was about to be turned up in my life.

We sat down and talked, and I just "beat around the bush" in regards to some things. He asked me to fill out some papers regarding this other information that I had previously shared with him. I did not say anything to him concerning the police due to the detective that was present with him. After they left, I thought to myself, "Now what do I do?" About a week later I called the same agent again and made arrangements to meet with him out of town. At this point I talked to him about the officers that I had information about and gave him a couple of names, including the name of the accountant, and a person that sat on the city council.

—Thirteen—
My First Time Getting Busted

A couple of weeks went by and it was business as usual. I was still dealing, using drugs, and numbering my days. I continued to read the Bible from time to time, but all seemed hopeless. You see, I did not know how to ask God to help me. I thought it was up to me to get myself out of this mess. After all, it was the decisions I had made that got me here. I remember one day, as I was counting money and getting ready to make a drop, I heard a voice saying, "I am losing you." I took this as the voice of God. My response was, "I know what I am doing!" Now I thank God that He winks at our ignorance during times like this. Things were very confusing for me and I really thought it was up to me to figure things out. Reader let me give you some personal advice. Never tell God that you know what you are doing!

I was beginning to be overcome with despair. Now, more than ever, I felt so alone. I had been up for days. My car would not start and I had to meet with a friend. I had shut my home phone off and was just using my cell phone at the time, but my battery was dead. I got on my bike and road down to make a phone call at the 7-Eleven; and at the same time, meet with the boss to give him some money. When I got there he had the same guy in his car that I had seen before. I was sure that this was the one they decided to bring in to "clean things up." He told me to put my bike in the back and he would give me a ride. He asked me where the rest of the last drop was and I told him that I still had most of it at home. I told him "no thanks," on the ride and that he could meet me at my house where we could talk more. I knew if I would have gotten into that car, I might not have made it home!

When I arrived back at home, I just sat down to think. I knew things were coming to an end. The friend I called had still not arrived and I needed to call her back. At this time I started to hear some very strange things. It was the spirits talking to me. This was so weird; I got on my bike and started to ride down the street. I stopped at a house a few blocks away and knocked on the door. I was going to ask to use their phone. I did not know them and why I happened to stop there I may never understand. No one came to the door. The spirits started talking to me again saying, "You see this new jeep, it is yours, take it; the keys are in it." I happened to look over and saw that they had left their keys in their new jeep. I looked around, left my bike, and took it. I went back to my house, picked up a few things, and decided to go see my son. Perhaps it would be the last time I might see him.

When things had started to get really deep, I had told his mother it would be best if he just stayed with her. I kind of explained things to her, but all she did was get really mad. I don't blame her, she just wanted me to get it together and be there for my son. No one around me knew the whole story of what was going on in my life. I had never shared it with anyone either. (I still cannot tell everything, for I realize that certain things are just better if never spoken about again.)

My son lived in Michigan, just about 10 minutes over the state line. I only lived about 5 minutes south of the Indiana state line. When I got to the main road, about a half a mile down, I passed a county police officer. He turned around and started to chase me. I had 2 ounces of meth on me, so I shoved it under the dash and figured it would be best if I just pulled over. After pulling over, I got out of the vehicle. Immediately, the officer drew his weapon and told me to get on the ground; he then put the gun to my head and called for backup. I stayed in that position until backup came. I was quickly hand-cuffed and put in the squad car.

As the officers were conversing with one another, I was being tormented by the evil spirits telling me that plans were now being made to eliminate my son and his mother. At that moment, a pick-up truck that was pulling a trailer full of wood went by and the spirits said to me, "You see that pile of wood in that truck? They're going to get your son and burn him!" In my mind I believed this because of all the things I was involved in. I was about to go nuts! Then a Michigan State police officer pulled up and they put me in his car. What I did not realize was that I had just made it over the state line and was now out of Indiana jurisdiction. The officers never searched the vehicle, they just looked through the few things I had on the seat. They never found the drugs.

As I look back on things, I realize God never left me. He was always there working in a very mysterious way. He saved my life a couple of times that day. I do believe that the drug ring I was involved in was going to put me down that day. Had I made the wrong move, I believe the officer holding his weapon on me would have shot me. On top of this, had they searched the vehicle, they would have found the drugs, which would have been enough to put me away for 20 to 30 years.

I was taken to a county jail in Michigan. While I sat there in my cell I was told by a soft-spoken voice to just keep looking up. I believe this was my guardian angel trying to get me to call on Jesus for help, but I did not understand. I started to get really cold and asked one of the officers for a blanket, but they refused to give me one. I began to get very angry. I wanted to make a phone call and they would not help me with that either. One of the officers started to make fun of me and I snapped. I punched the glass window and told him to come on in and I would do him some harm. (Of course I used different language.)

I then told him I wanted to see a nurse because I was not feeling well. A nurse came and gave me some aspirin. Later, the head officer came and talked with me. He evaluated the situation and decided to get me further medical treatment. They had me taken to the state hospital. I stayed there for 3 weeks and went through detox, followed by a trip back to the county jail.

Soon I was taken to court. The judge looked sternly at me and asked what I was thinking about; why at my age, with no criminal record, why would I be doing something like this. My reply was, "Your Honor, I have a drug problem and I need some help." He told me that there are other ways of getting help. I told him I needed help now. Of course, I did not fill him in on the details. He gave me time served with a $400.00 fine and six months probation.

I was sent back to the county jail where I was informed that I would not be released because there was a hold on me. What I did not know, was that the Secret Service and the local police force <u>both</u> put holds on me. About an hour later I asked if I could go for a walk in the gym to stretch my legs. The officer looked at me and asked, "Don't you want to go home?" I thought she was being smart with me. They had just told me that there was a hold on me and I was not going to be released. I said, "Sure," and to my surprise the officers hurried me out of the facility and sent me on my way. I certainly did not understand the conflicting statements, but I was in no position to question them.

—FOURTEEN—
Back to the Same Old Thing

I hitch-hiked home, called my drug dealer, and met with him. Of course, he was upset with everything. I owed him a lot of money, lost the last batch of dope that he gave me, and I had no money at that time to give him. He told me that was it; I was getting nothing else from him and that he wanted his money! Within two days I made an insurance claim on my house for some water damage from the winter before, picked up a check, and went to someone else who I knew was getting drugs from the same people. I picked up a batch, made contact with an old friend, and moved across town to start over again, but on a smaller scale. I picked up a car from a friend who had a used car lot, and was back in business … for myself.

Oddly, I started reading the Bible again. I told God that I just wanted to go somewhere and get away from everything. Again, I was trying to do everything myself. (The biggest mistake we make in life is to think we have the ability to change ourselves!)

About a week later I called Agent John to see if he wanted to meet again and talk. He seemed to be upset. I still did not know at this time that the Secret Service had a hold on me. He asked me where I was calling from, but I refused to tell him. He became angrier with me and told me that he was going to get me that he would find me! I took this as a threat and hung up. I thought to myself, "I am in more trouble than I can imagine."

I kept turning to humans for help and not God. I still hadn't figured out that He would help me, or how to ask Him for help. So I placed a call to someone in the CIA, thinking that I just had to go up higher on the chain. I explained the situation regarding Agent John who was with the Secret Service, how he had brought an officer to my house after I made it clear not to approach me with any local authorities because I was concerned with the President's safety and that I had reason to believe that something might happen to him. I explained that I was sharing information with Agent John, and that now during our last conversation he had just made a threat to me over the phone. I shared some other things with this agent and answered some question he had asked. I then told this agent that if anything was to happen to my family or me I would assassinate Agent John and any other officers involved.

He asked if I was in a safe place and I told him I did not feel safe anywhere. He asked me for the phone number that I was calling from and if I would wait there for about 20 minutes. He would have someone call me right back. About 20 minutes later the phone rang and it was an agent with the Secret Service in Washington, D. C. We talked about what was going on with my dispute with Agent John. I told him to check the phone records at the federal building and to listen to our conversation in which he would hear Agent John threaten me. At this time, this agent told me that he would contact me later if they needed more information.

You see, Agent John was in charge of setting up security for the President when he came to this area. When he was told to come and see me by those above him, he did so; but as Agent John was gathering information on me from the local authorities he was not sharing this info with those at the main office.

I went back to my friend's house and for the next couple of days started to drink very heavily. I was going down hill fast. For some reason I decided to call Agent John back. He seemed to be nice to me over the phone and told me that he was wondering what had happened with me. He said that a couple of other agents were coming up from down-state and wanted to talk with me. I told him to have the agent call me when they got into town. The next day John called asking me to meet with him the following day.

Upon my arrival at the meeting place, Agent John approached me and introduced Agent Dave. At that time Agent Dave asked me if I was hungry and invited me to have lunch with them so we could talk. He then told Agent John to head over to a nearby restaurant and we walked over. On our walk he asked me what was going on and I filled him in briefly. After we ordered our meal, we sat down in a booth away from people. The first thing out of Agent John was, "You threatened to kill me?" I said, "Yes, I did, but I did not mean it. I was just upset with the way you initially approached me." He then said to me, "You seem to be pretty resourceful. You just got out of jail, you're wearing new clothes, and driving a new car; besides this, the Secret Service and the local police had a hold on you; but you were released, and we did not so much as get a phone call."

I knew at this moment they were very curious about whom I knew that could give an override on a Secret Service hold. Then Agent Dave started asking me questions pertaining to my military background. I decided to tell Agent Dave the truth. Of course, he did not believe me. With nothing on record other than my enlistment papers and some pay records there was no way of knowing if I had been telling the truth. With the way everything appeared, I had done more than that for the government. So, I let their imaginations run wild. I then talked with him about the local officers and the things they were involved in. After the meeting, Agent Dave said he would be in touch and we went our separate ways.

About a week later, Agent Dave called me and asked me to meet with him that evening. I was partying at a friend's house and told him I would meet with him the next day. That night I was really drunk, and I was alone at my friend's house. I was reflecting back on my life and broke down and began to cry. For the first time I asked God to help me; I told God that I did not want to go down this road any more. I had finally burnt out. I had hit bottom. I would just as soon die than to keep living the way I was. The answer to my prayer came within 24 hours. The next day, when I met with Agent Dave, I was arrested and indicted on the charge of threatening to assassinate and/or murder a federal officer. Praise God for deliverance! I sure didn't expect it like this!

Reader, don't ever think that God does not hear your prayers. He is forever reaching out to help us. We often are looking for His help in a way that we want, for our own selfish reasons. God knows the best way of helping us in <u>every</u> situation! My friend, no mater what you are struggling with Jesus Christ is willing to help you right now.

In the Bible is a story of the disciples of Jesus crossing a sea on a boat. The waves were rough and the wind was against them. They saw what they thought was a spirit and cried out in fear. But Jesus spoke to them and said, *"Be of good cheer; it is I; be not afraid."* And His disciple Peter said, *"Lord, if it be Thou, bid me come unto Thee on the water. And Jesus said, "come."* And when Peter came down out of the ship, he walked on the water, toward Jesus. But when he saw the wind blowing very hard, he was afraid; and beginning to sink, he cried, saying, *"Lord, save me."* Now please note what the Word of God says next. *"And <u>immediately</u> Jesus stretched forth His hand, and caught him."* See *Matthew 14:24–31.*

This is what happened to me; Jesus caught me! So I ask you to please right now—ask Him to save you. No matter how rough things may look, no matter how dim the situation may seem, no matter how bad you may feel, I encourage you to just cry out, "Jesus save me!" He died on the cross for you and more. It is His delight to stretch forth His hand and catch you. But you must be willing to accept the help that

He is offering. For me it was prison, and yes it took me just a little bit of time to recognize this; but when I did I praised His name and continue to do so to this day!

—FIFTEEN—
My Time in Court

I went before the Federal court and they decided that I should have a psychological examination, so they sent me to the east coast to a prison in Massachusetts. There I spent the next six weeks. During this time, I began to read the Bible diligently. I would spend all day just reading; I was searching to understand what God wanted with me. I began to read the Bible as if my name was in there somewhere. As I reflected on my life and the way God made Himself known to me, I thought I had to be in there somewhere.

Reader, what I found out later was that we are all in there. All through the Bible you will read of people that had similar character traits as yourself. There were murderers, liars, prostitutes, gossipers, proud and arrogant people as well, and many more. Some of these people where delivered from their evil ways. They chose to be saved. Others chose to continue to rebel and in the end reaped what they sowed. Know this, that if we don't get to go home when Jesus comes it is because we have chosen a different course and refuse to let Him save us.

During the day and in the evening from time to time I would share and read with other inmates. There were a few others that were also studying. I was kept locked down in one area and was only permitted to go outside occasionally. Most of the time when everyone else went outside I would just stay inside and enjoy the peace and quiet. When I did go outside we were confined to a small area that was boxed in with three walls and a fifteen foot fence. It was refreshing to go outside though and get some sunlight and fresh air.

After about 5 weeks, I sat down with a doctor and he began to ask me a bunch of questions. He would ask me to repeat things we had just talked about. Then came the big question, "Mr. Page what did you do in the military?" I knew then that the Secret Service was still inquiring into my military training and orders. I told the doctor I was a combat engineer. He then asked me if I ever killed anyone. I told him that this information was confidential. He then asked me if I ever killed anyone using explosives, again I told him that this was confidential. By this time he was outraged and yelled at me and told me that if I did not answer these questions that he would hold me incompetent. I told him "Fine."

About a week later I was sent back to court and my attorney objected to the claim the doctor had made. He felt that I was competent and that I understood the charges pending against me. My attorney then requested that I be re-evaluated. The prosecutor agreed but told my attorney that he would have to pay for it. After the last go around with the psychologist, I figured it would be best if I prayed and asked God to help me. This was the beginning of many times that I would learn to surrender to God and let Him lead. I met with this doctor and he began the questioning … one question after another for about an hour and a half. He was going through a book and was recording my answers.

A couple of days later I called my attorney to get the update on the doctor's reply. He told me that the doctor found me to be competent, and that I got a perfect score on the test. My attorney told me that the doctor told him that nobody has ever received a perfect score on this test before. Praise God, for He is able to do great things in our lives if we just surrender all to Him.

—Sixteen—
God Begins to Teach Me Himself

During all this I still read the Scriptures diligently, but it was very difficult to focus. I would have to read the same passage over and over. My mind was consistently thinking about something else while reading. There was seldom a quiet moment. There were 24 inmates in our unit, and it was set up with two-man cells. With everything that was going on, it seemed almost hopeless to try to read the Bible and understand what I was reading. I was now reading it through for the second time.

There always seemed to be someone that would give their explanation on what the Scriptures were saying; but I did not want to listen to anyone. I heard all kinds of things such as how the Ten Commandments didn't matter or how some of them do and some don't; how Jesus is going to come and take certain people and leave some behind to face the plagues that are spoken of in Revelation, how those "left behind" would have a second chance, how you would burn in hell forever and ever … and on and on. I even read a book that another inmate shared with me called *Left Behind*. After reading it I knew then I would never get the truth from man. It was time to call on the name of the Lord.

Reader, I would like to share this poem with you that I wrote at a time in need.

Please Jesus Let Me Not Go Astray

I get down on my knees and begin to pray.
Dear Jesus, help me this day, I am surrounded by darkness that is trying to carry me away, please Jesus let me not go astray.

Teach me your words of wisdom; bless me with knowledge and understanding in a special way.
Show me how to fight off the darkness that seeks to consume me this day. Let it not have victory over me, for I cannot praise Thee from the grave.
I thirst for Thy righteousness and cry out for Thy strength.
Let Thy light shine on my path and guide my way.
Oh, please, Jesus, let me not go astray.
I need Thee in my life each and every day, for Thou are my life.
Thou are eternal light and the only way to the everlasting world that I hope to go to some day.
So please Jesus let me not go astray.

I then found my comfort in the Word of God.

"The LORD [is] good, a strong hold in the day of trouble; and He knoweth them that trust in Him." Nahum 1:7

"Be not afraid of their faces: for I [am] with thee to deliver thee, saith the LORD." Jeremiah 1:8

"And thou, son of man, be not afraid of them, neither be afraid of their words, though briers and thorns [be] with thee, and thou dost dwell among scorpions: be not afraid of their words, nor be dismayed at their looks, though they [be] a rebellious house." Ezekiel 2:6

"For I the LORD thy God will hold thy right hand, saying unto thee, Fear not; I will help thee." Isaiah 41:13

I remember reading a passage in the Gospel of John:

"And I will pray the Father, and He shall give you another Comforter, that He may abide with you for ever …

But the Comforter, [which is] the Holy Ghost, Whom the Father will send in My name, He shall teach you all things, and bring all things to your remembrance, whatsoever I have said unto you." John 14:16, 26

And then in the book of *I John,* it all became clear:

"But the anointing which ye have received of Him abideth in you, and ye need not that any man teach you: but as the same anointing teacheth you of all things, and is truth, and is no lie, and even as it hath taught you, ye shall abide in Him." I John 2:27

There it was God's promise to teach me. Not only me, but you, the reader of this book as well, if you just ask.

So I prayed and asked God to teach me and for me to have some alone time with Him. Within a week I got my alone time. I had gotten into a dispute with some other inmates and was sent to solitary confinement for the next three weeks.

Here I had a time of deep reflection and my heart was weighed down greatly. Someone had shared a little pamphlet with me, and I was deeply moved by it. It was about a little boy that was living in the streets. He was cold, hungry, and alone. With nobody to help him, all he wanted was for someone to return to him the love that he shared with others. I was then moved to write this poem as I thought about what he must have been feeling. In a way it reminded me of myself and my search as a child.

Crying Out

My God, my God, I cry out. How much longer will it be, before all the love that I have poured out comes back to me?
Will I walk alone in this world for eternity?

Please my God, answer, how long will it be?
As my cup has run dry time and time again, I am truly grateful as Thy Son has filled me up within.
But I must say the sorrow in my heart grows great and the pain in my soul now overflows like a river into the sea.
Can Thou not see? The pain and sorrow that now floods the shores are the feelings that pour out of me.
Could it be by chance this is how my life is to be?
Alone and destitute of sorrow for eternity.
I know life is but a vapor, only here for a moment and then blows away like dust in the wind.
So I plea with Thee, my Father, my Savior, my Friend, will Thou embrace me in the end?

How many children and adults in the world cry out these same words? At times our lives seem like a road of sorrow and loneliness. When the pain and despair seems to be all you can embrace, know that there is hope and uplifting in the Word of God. Jesus Christ has made a pledge with us to give us the strength and comfort we need in the most difficult times. For His words of promise are:

> *"... I will never leave thee, nor forsake thee." Hebrews 13:5*

> *"... and, lo, I am with you alway, [even] unto the end of the world." Matthew 28:20*

When our hearts melt away with fear and we feel crushed with despair, remember:

> *"The LORD [is] nigh unto them that are of a broken heart; and saveth such as be of a contrite spirit." Psalm 34:18*

I cried out to the Lord in my suffering, and He heard me; and my friend, he will hear you too.

> *"Be of good courage, and He shall strengthen your heart, all ye that hope in the Lord." Psalm 31:24*

> *"Blessed [are] they that mourn: for they shall be comforted." Matthew 5:4*

After my time in solitary confinement, I was moved to another unit. Now the inmate that was in the cell with me was named Paul. We would sit up late every night reading and sharing with each other. Then one day he said to me, "Look, I have some of these studies here under my mattress that I have been doing called *Amazing Facts.* They're Bible Studies based on Biblical facts only; I think you would like them."

So I started to read these small pamphlets that were only about 12–15 pages long. Each one was based on a Biblical topic and they would build on one another. As I began to read my first study which was entitled, *"Is There Anything Left You Can Trust?"* I was amazed; God answered my prayer completely. It was God teaching me through His written Word. Any question I had, sooner or later, I received an answer to, such as: Are the dead really dead? Is the Devil in charge of hell? What will heaven be like? Who is the antichrist? What is the mark of the beast? What is the sin God cannot forgive? This Bible study also took me through the books of *Daniel* and *Revelation* allowing the Bible to interpret itself. What a blessing!

Reader, if you are tired of the confusion and the opinions of man, if you're tired of being lied to and are to the point that you aren't sure just what to believe, then I encourage you to send off for the Bible studies now. It's free and they will change your life. Your walk with God will be strengthened and your faith will increase greatly as you read these Biblical facts for yourself. (See page 150 of this book for information to send off for your free Bible Studies.)

—SEVENTEEN—
Back to Court

Now it was back to court where my attorney presented everything to the judge. The prosecutor was not pleased at all and denied the results. She insisted that I be re-examined again at the government's expense. She was determined to get her way proving that I was mentally incapable of understanding what was taking place. Again I prayed, "God help me."

I was taken by the federal marshals to a nearby clinic. One of the marshals and I went into the office and sat down. The doctor took a minute and looked over my file. Then he wrote out a prescription and told the marshal to bring me back in 6 weeks. The marshal then told the doctor that I was there for an evaluation. He looked through his file again and began to question me. He asked me what I had done. I told him I had threatened to kill a federal agent. He asked, "Why?" I told him that I felt the agent put my life in danger during a period of time when I was giving him information. The agent had brought an officer to my house from the force that I had been speaking against. He then told the marshal that he was finished. The marshal was shocked, he knew as well as I did that these evaluations lasted much longer that this and when we got in the hallway, he told me that he would call my attorney, the prosecutor, and the federal probation department and let them know what had happened. Praise God for a witness. At a later date, the marshal made a statement in the court in regards to the length of time of the evaluation.

I was taken back to my cell and I knew the odds were piling up against me. All I wanted was a fair evaluation. Needless to say, I was in despair. After a couple days went by everything seemed to be weighing me down, I missed my son and I just wanted to go home. But where would I go? I had lost everything.

Then one night the most beautiful promise came to me. I was deep in sleep and I heard a soft voice tell me, "Read *Deuteronomy 1:30,*" I woke up and thought to myself, "that was strange." I tried to go back to sleep but I could not. I kept hearing this passage. I felt a strong impression to get up and read this passage. I did not understand this, I never heard God talk to me like this before. I climbed down from the top bunk and opened my Bible to *Deuteronomy 1:30*:

> *"The LORD your God which goeth before you, He shall fight for you, according to all that He did for you in Egypt before your eyes."*

Wow! I was amazed. I thought to myself "I'm not in Egypt," so I went back and read the story of the Exodus and how God helped His children. What a beautiful story, what a loving God, and what a wonderful promise.

A couple days later I got a copy of the last doctor report. It was terrible! He said that I was delusional, very violent that I should be under close supervision and under medication at all times; and that I was a danger to society! I thought to myself, "what now?" When I went back to court my attorney totally objected to this evaluation. How could a person come up with all this from a few questions during an 8 minute conversation? I was calm through the whole ordeal. The courts then decided to subpoena the first two doctors to court and have them argue their points as to whether I was competent.

The night before the hearing the doctor from the Massachusetts Federal Prison which was first to say that I was incompetent, called my attorney and told him that he had a change of mind and now agreed that I was competent. The next day at court when questioned about why he changed his mind the doctor said that after several conversations with my attorney he decided that I was competent and decided to withdraw his first statement. God was working. Finally there was no objection and a sentencing date was set.

After a few weeks my attorney came to see me and told me that the prosecutor for the US government was offering me a 5-year plea agreement with an open end. This meant that if I accepted I would be in agreement with them giving me 5 years and the open-end meant I would be accepting additional time if the judge felt I needed it. I could do this or go to trial. I decided to sign the papers. After appearing in court and giving my guilty plea I felt some relief. You see, it did not matter anymore to me if I did 5 years or 20 years. I belonged to God and I had made the decision that whatever happened I would serve Jesus Christ. I'd like to share a Scripture reading with you from *Psalms 102:16–20:*

> *"When the Lord shall build up Zion, He shall appear in His glory. He will regard the prayer of the destitute, and not despise their prayer. This shall be written for the generation to come: and the people which shall be created shall praise the Lord. For He hath looked down from the height of His sanctuary; from heaven did the Lord behold the earth; To hear the groaning of the prisoner; to loose those that are appointed to death."*

Do you feel destitute; do you feel that there is no way out of the situation that you are in or facing? Direct your prayer to the Lord, share with Him everything and allow Him to guide your life and direct your path.

On the way back to the jail after pleading guilty, one of the marshals asked me how it went. I told him that I pleaded guilty to a 5 year open. He was shocked. You see these marshals have witnessed many open-end agreements and most of the time the prisoner gets more time. I told him I had faith.

He said, "I do too, but not that much." I have come to understand that there are those that have a basic understanding of faith as to say they believe what the Bible says; and then there are those that have faith not only because they believe what the Bible says, but have a day to day experience with God and Jesus Christ. Therefore, their faith is alive and growing through reading and living the Word. It has become a real part of their lives. How about you? Has it become a real part of your life? Do you believe the promises of God as well as believe that He is able to fulfill His word?

—EIGHTEEN—
My Last Day at Court

It was time to go before the judge. On my way into court my attorney pulled me aside and told me that the judge said that I could pick the prison I wanted to go to as long as it was a medical facility. Now this sounded strange to me. I thought to myself, "Now what are they up to."

Now it was time. The judge addressed me, "Mr. Page, will you please stand. Do you have anything you would like to say?" "Yes your Honor, throughout this case I have been re-evaluated several times and all that I have ever wanted was a fair evaluation. My request is that if I am to be evaluated again that no other evaluations that have been done in the past be viewed so that the person doing the evaluation would do so without any preconceived ideas; and I ask that you do not court order me to be put on any medication. I have been on drugs most of my life and I don't want to be on a different drug now."

The judge said that he would not give me this choice in regards to my other records being viewed upon further evaluations. He then said, "Mr. Page has your attorney explained to you that you may pick the prison you want to go to?" "Yes, your honor, he told me that Rochester, Minnesota was a nice place. So I choose to go there." The judge agreed and told me while I was there I was to get another evaluation. Then he said, "I am sentencing you to 21 months." My heart was racing. I was shocked! All I could say was, "thank you;" and I have been praising God every since.

Dear reader let us never forget that Jesus Christ is our mediator.

"For we have not an High Priest which cannot be touched with the feeling of our infirmities; but was in all points tempted like as [we are, yet] without sin. Let us therefore come boldly unto the throne of grace, that we may obtain mercy, and find grace to help in time of need." Hebrews 4:15, 16

"For [there is] one God, and one mediator between God and men, the Man Christ Jesus." I Timothy 2:5

Let us always understand even though the enemy joins hand in hand and all we see is a wall of opposition before us, and Satan continuing to increase the darkness around us remember this:

"With him [is] an arm of flesh; but with us [is] the LORD our God to help us, and to fight our battles." II Chronicles 32:8

During my case, I had made some accusations against some police officers in the area and all the prosecutor kept saying was that I was fabricating; as I was going through my case some of these officers where being brought up on charges that were matching up with what I had been saying. So again the Scriptures prove what they say:

"For God shall bring every work into judgment, with every secret thing, whether [it be] good, or whether [it be] evil." Ecclesiastes 12:14

"For nothing is secret, that shall not be made manifest; neither [any thing] hid, that shall not be known and come abroad." Luke 8:17

For all things will be known whether they be found out before we die or when we stand before God as our Judge. For even the secret things of the heart that we think are never to be known, are open to the eyes of the Lord. Let us not fool ourselves, for God knows the heart and the imagination of our thoughts:

> *"For the LORD searcheth all hearts, and understandeth all the imaginations of the thoughts." I Chronicles 28:9*

—Nineteen—
My Time in the Federal Prison

On arriving at my final destination it was time to be processed. I was told that I would be on a landscape work detail there at the prison. When I walked into the prison I felt at peace. It was, as my attorney said, a very nice place. There were fruit trees and beautiful flowers everywhere. They even had their own vegetable garden. There was some wild life like, hawks, squirrels, and geese. There was a nice outside track and a very nice chapel.

I first went directly to my cell to put up my things and took my Bible out into the yard to read. It was a blessing just to touch the grass. Oh, how everything looked so much brighter now. The tress waving in the wind, the beautiful flowers were blooming, the fluffy clouds in the sky, all creation giving praise to God.

It was not long before another inmate came up to me and asked, "Do you understand what you're reading there?" I told him, 'Yes" and that I was still searching. So he sat down and we began to talk. I knew right away he was anxious to teach me. But, you see, I already had a teacher, the Holy Spirit. I was holding onto God's promises in His Word. Jesus said:

> *"If ye love Me, keep My commandments. And I will pray the Father, and He shall give you another Comforter, that He may abide with you for ever." John 14:15, 16*

Here is a beautiful promise but there is a condition, one must love Jesus, and we show this love by keeping His Commandments. It is only by accepting the grace and the divine influence upon our hearts that this is accomplished. Jesus said:

"He that hath My Commandments, and keepeth them, he it is that loveth Me: and he that loveth Me shall be loved of My Father, and I will love him, and will manifest Myself to him ... If a man love Me, he will keep My words: and My Father will love him, and we will come unto him, and make our abode with him." John 14:21, 23

These passages bring me joy. How about you?

But there is more, Jesus goes on to say:

"But the Comforter, [which is] the Holy Ghost, whom the Father will send in My name, He shall teach you all things, and bring all things to your remembrance, whatsoever I have said unto you ... Howbeit when He, the Spirit of truth, is come, He will guide you into all truth: for He shall not speak of Himself; but whatsoever He shall hear, [that] shall He speak: and He will show you things to come." John 14:26; 16:13

Now I understand that the Lord will give some the gift of teaching, but we are given abundant warning about false prophets and false teachers:

"But there were false prophets also among the people, even as there shall be false teachers among you, who privily shall bring in damnable heresies, even denying the Lord that bought them, and bring upon themselves swift destruction. And many shall follow their pernicious ways; by reason of whom the way of truth shall be evil spoken of." II Peter 2:1–2

I know that there are a lot of God fearing people out there that are searching for the truth, and enjoy sharing the light they have received. This does not necessarily qualify them as teachers of the Word. As I have experienced, many times when they come to a part in the Scriptures that they do not fully comprehend they permit pride to rise up in their hearts and feel they have the wisdom to interpret what it means; or often they explain it the way that they have heard it from someone else, perhaps their parents. A lot of the time they are sharing what they have heard a pastor or minister explain. Even a lot of these pastors or ministers and even parents are so set in their ways that they close the door to their own hearts to receive true light and; therefore, preach and teach a lie.

Dear readers, the Scriptures are our only safeguard. All that come to Jesus and asks Him to teach them, His Word promises to do so. Jesus said:

> *"I am the bread of life: he that cometh to Me shall never hunger; and he that believeth on Me shall never thirst … All that the Father giveth Me shall come to Me; and him that cometh to Me I will in no wise cast out." John 6:35, 37*

Now I was told that I had 2 weeks to find a job at the prison. I was to go around and fill out applications just as I would do on the outside. I also was told that all the new people get assigned to kitchen duty. But I told the inmates that said this to me that the officer at the gate told me that I would be working in landscaping. They just laughed. So I waited until a couple of days went by before my time was up, and went to the landscape office and filled out my application, got an interview, and was told to report to work the following Monday. Praise God!

Each day after cutting the grass I would just sit there and read my little pocket Bible. I also enjoyed reading a book called *Steps to Christ*, and *The Desire of Ages*; both are well written books by an inspired author. I also enjoyed being outside in nature, looking upon God's creation. I remember being so thankful for just being able to sit on the soft green grass. I had never before stopped to look upon our Father's creation as I did now. Everything looked so much brighter than I remembered it. The area I worked in had plum trees and sometimes when the fruit was ripe I would pick some and enjoy the fresh taste.

As I was writing this last paragraph I was deeply reflecting on these moments and I began to cry. I thought about the grace that has been given to me and I realized that I don't want to hurt Jesus anymore, for He suffered enough. I knew some that were killed or died never accepting the love or grace of our Everlasting Father. How about you? Are you grateful for the grace that you have received? As long as you are alive and breathing Jesus is knocking at the door of your heart. Will you let Him in? This place is not our home; Jesus has a much better place for us if we would just let Him come into our hearts He will make the change.

During my time at the Federal Prison, I studied diligently and searched the Scriptures daily. I would fellowship with others but I refused to accept anything but the Bible Truth. I finished with my *Amazing Facts* studies and started another study called, *The Storacles of Prophecy*. Again, it was based upon Biblical facts only and allowed the Bible to interpret itself.

During my stay, I would from time to time like to play a game of chess. There was one person in particular that I enjoyed playing against, even though I lost most of the time. His name was Chuck Gibson. He was restricted to a wheelchair and only had the full use of his left hand. He was kind of a wild looking guy, but I noticed how kind he was to others, always sharing whatever he had and if there was something that he could do for you he would happily do it. During our games, I would talk to him about Jesus and I would share with him how God had done so many things for me; how He was teaching me through His Word some really amazing things. But he did not want to hear it. This was a very touchy subject. Sometimes he would start using profane language and tell me to stop talking about it. He told me one time how angry he was and if God was a loving God, he wanted to know why did He put him in a wheelchair, and why did God kill his brothers?

Chuck had been in an accident at the age of nineteen and from the results of that he was paralyzed from his chest down. Also, later in life, he lost a couple of brothers. I told him that God did not put him in that wheelchair, or kill his brothers; nor did He put us in prison. I told him this was all the results of sin. It was because of the choices we made in life to indulge in sinful activity and these are the consequences. He did not want to hear that either.

Chuck would attend a pagan worship service. They worshiped 36 different gods! But I never gave up. One day I was sharing with him some things out of the Book of *Daniel* about the four beasts in chapter seven: how four beasts would came up from the sea, diverse one from another. How each beast represented a kingdom, how they would succeed one another, and how the last one would be divided up. I shared with him that through a careful study of history one could see that the Bible was right in line with the events that have taken place. The Bible even gave very accurate dates in which certain things would happen; they had been fulfilled right on time with yet a few remaining. Now this seemed to interest him. He even shared with someone in his worship group and then asked the whole group if they would be willing to listen to what I had shared with him. Of course he was ridiculed and they did not have anything pleasant to say about me either. He stopped going to that service for a while but later returned. Chuck and I bonded in a great friendship even though we had different religious beliefs.

Every chance possible I would share the *Amazing Facts* studies with others. It was my desire to see people come to the knowledge of the truth. I started attending a Tuesday night worship service from time to time as I was searching for direction from God. I came to learn from the Scriptures that the Bible spoke of a Sabbath day, which was special to God's people. In the fourth commandment it is written:

> *"Remember the Sabbath day, to keep it holy. Six days shalt thou labour, and do all thy work: But the seventh day [is] the Sabbath of the LORD thy God: [in it] thou shalt not do any work, thou, nor thy son, nor thy daughter, thy manservant, nor thy maidservant, nor thy cattle, nor thy stranger that [is] within thy gates: For [in] six days the LORD made heaven and earth, the sea, and all that in them [is], and rested the seventh day: wherefore the LORD blessed the Sabbath day, and hallowed it." Exodus 20:8–11*

Now as I continued to read the Scriptures, I noticed that the Sabbath day was mentioned quite a bit. I believe it is mentioned over 150 times, so I realized it must be important. I first read about it in the Book of *Genesis 2:2, 3*, how God made the seventh day a day of rest; and that He, as the Creator of the world, sanctified it. Then I read about it in *Exodus 16:22–30*. Then in *Exodus 20:8-11,* and of course it is the fourth Commandment. I noticed that these laws applied to all that did abide in the camp; for there was a mixed multitude that left Egypt with them. (See *Exodus 12:38.*) This is why when God gave the Ten Commandments He mentioned the stranger in the fourth commandment. All through the Bible I saw how Israel got in a lot of trouble with God for not keeping His Commandments, especially the Sabbath.

So I started to wonder if there was a Sabbath service at the prison so that I could worship on the seventh day according to God's Word. I also became interested in how Sunday worship came about. I had never read anything in the Bible that mentioned Sunday worship. Later God revealed this to me as well. (Please see page 130 in regards to Biblical day of worship—Saturday or Sunday.)

I found that there was a worship service on Saturday and I was glad to join in. The name of the church was called Seventh Day Adventist. I had never heard of them before; but everything I was hearing at the service was in harmony with the Scriptures, and I liked that. Many of times when I attended other religious services some of the things I was hearing seemed contrary to what the Scriptures taught. Plus, I did not learn very much from them.

During my stay at the federal prison, I met some very devoted Christians. Another inmate that I became good friends with was a man named Berga Smith, an ex-gang-member and drug dealer out of Chicago. I shared the *Amazing Facts* studies with him and we would talk about Jesus all the time. He would always take care of me if I got hungry between meals. Often with my favorite treat, a candy bar. We stay in close touch and I can't wait to see him when he gets out.

On my departure date I said good bye to my two new best friends. They were true friends that shared kindness and love and looked for nothing in return. I could see Jesus Christ in both of them, even my friend Chuck, who did not know Jesus as a personal Saviour. Tears were shed and I know they both thought in their hearts that they probably would never hear from me again. That is how it is about ninety percent of the time when someone gets released; they never write back or visit. But I knew that these two men would be my friends for life.

Reader, if you are in prison reading this book. I appeal to you, those that you truly bond with, don't let them down when you get out, stay in touch; or if you're somebody that knows someone that is incarcerated, it would truly be a blessing to them if you would take the time to write once in a while. People in prison are human beings too. We all have sinned and come short of the glory of God. (*Romans 3:23*)

—TWENTY—
My Stay at the Halfway House

A halfway house is a place that is used at times where they release prisoners to once they have served their time. It is a chance to prove that you are able to adapt into society. I was to stay there for the next six weeks.

Upon my arrival I called my son Travis and told him that it would not be long now. I did not want to give him a date because most of my life I failed to keep appointments in a timely manner, and I wasn't exactly sure even after I was released when I would be able to see him. After talking to his mother, I could see she was a little hesitant to let me right back into his life, but I understood why; she was looking out for his best interest. She had no idea of my conversion experience. There was no way for me to prove to her I had changed. All I could do was to be patient and hope that in time she would see the new me. This was going to be a challenge because I wanted so much to get right back into my son's life.

I told her that I understood why she did not trust me, and I knew it would take time. After talking to her she came to visit me and brought me some new clothes and a very nice coat. Even though I caused her much pain, she still showed me compassion and love in all my times of need. Throughout my whole case she accepted all my phone calls, sent me money when needed, and also sent me some nice cards. I thank God for her, for she was the last person I thought would be there for me, but she was throughout the whole experience.

My next phone call was to Pastor Wayne Morrison. I had written him just before I left prison. He wrote back, gave me his phone number and told me to call him when I arrived in the area. He did not delay; he came right over with one of the elders. They made arrangements for me to be picked up every Sabbath. I really enjoyed the services and sharing my experiences with God. Bob and Missy Stringer were the elders of the Church that I attended in Michigan City. They were very kind and had me over as often as I could come for fellowship meal.

Even here at the halfway house I saw the opportunity to share the *Amazing Facts* studies with other inmates and even some of the staff. I remember a time back at the prison that one of the officers noticed these little booklets in my room and picked one up and started reading it. He took some back to his office and read them, and when he returned them I was very happy to see his interest. I shared all that I could with him and prayed for him as well. I started to notice how people were interested in the truth. So many people have been taught to believe a lie or have been deceived into believing tradition that when they receive the Biblical truth it really kindles a new desire to search the Scriptures.

—Twenty-one—

My Stay at the Homeless Shelter

It was time for me to leave the halfway house. I had just had my first meeting with my probation officer and he seemed to be nice. He made it clear that I would be seeing him once a week and that they would be keeping a very close eye on me. I thought to myself, "Good, maybe they will learn something about Jesus." He asked me if I had somewhere to go when I got out. I told him that my family did not want me around and I did not have any friends. For the first time in my life I realized nobody cared enough about me to even offer me a place to stay. Well, I knew God did, and that He would take care of things; so I started praying for my Lord Jesus Christ to make a way out of no way. He then asked me if I wanted to go back to my hometown. I told him, "No way!" There was no need for me to go back around all that chaos. I needed a fresh start, a new environment. The biggest mistake prisoners make when they get released is to go back to the same place where they first got into trouble. If you want to start a new life, you must change the people you hang around with and the places you stay and hang out; as well as the things you do and participate in. So many use the excuse that they have nowhere else to go. God will provide if you ask Him and are willing to go in the path that He directs you.

My probation officer asked me if I would stay at a homeless shelter in South Bend, Indiana. I told him yes. So he made some phone calls and they were kind enough to hold a bed for me, so the following week upon my release I would have a place to stay.

Well the day came, December 31, 2002, New Year's Eve. What a blessing to get out and start a new life right at the beginning of the year. My probation officer picked me up, gave me a ride to the shelter, and stayed with me while I got checked in. Again God had blessed. This place, from my understanding, was one of the nicest homeless shelters in the country. They not only provide you with a bed and food but there were many educational programs available. It was their goal to help people get back on their feet. At first I wanted to hurry up and get a job so that I could get back on my own and get my son back in my life, but God had another plan. This passage would often come to mind:

> *"Rest in the Lord, and wait patiently for Him." Psalms 37:7*

My lesson in patience was about to increase. I meet with Catherine, a case manager to discuss my goals. She was very nice and really wanted to help. She told me that it would be beneficial for me to go through the programs before looking for a job. The programs would only last about three months, so I agreed. Meanwhile I was able to do a little part time work in order to have a little money to do something with my son.

A week had passed, the Sabbath had come, and I wanted to go to church. I had a little directory sent to me from the Bible school which gave me a list of churches in the area. I noticed two churches on the map and recalled seeing one of the street names before. I figured it would be best if I walked to the church on Friday timing myself to see how long it would take. I did not want to miss out on any of the service. A person I met at the shelter agreed to go along. I never have been good with directions so it was up to God to guide my way. After walking about five blocks I thought we should have come across the street called Colfax by now, but I had gone in the wrong direction when I left the shelter. I should have turned left not right. I saw a street sign for Altgeld and I remember from my directory there was also a church on this street. We headed down that street, which had begun at that intersection, so there was only one way to go. After walking for about one hour it seemed we would never find it. My friend started saying that we should give up because on this street there was nothing but houses, but I was persistent, and shortly we came upon it. Little did I know we had walked to the next town called Mishawaka. Just as we arrived someone was pulling up and handed us a bulletin that showed the time of the services.

I was praising God all the way home. I could not wait to be there for my first Sabbath worship in my new church. The next morning my new friend and I started out again. Although it was very cold out, I knew the hour and half walk would be worth it. The service was great and we were blessed with a ride home. From that point on someone always picked me up and anybody else who wanted to go.

During my class at the homeless shelter called "Starting Over," we were studying about the brain and how it functions. I was learning that the brain is like a camera in that it takes pictures of what a person looks at then stores the image away. Later, you may recall these pictures and view it again in your mind. They used the illustration of dreaming. When you dream you see pictures and these are images you have possibly seen at one time or another in your life. These images often are replayed during sleep. Now of course many of people's dreams don't make any sense nor do you remember ever seeing some of the things you may dream about, but the whole illustration made a lot of sense to me.

One day I came across a Bible passage that stood out much clearer than ever before. It is a description of those that will be able to stand before God:

"He that walketh righteously, and speaketh uprightly; he that despiseth the gain of oppressions, that shaketh

his hands from holding of bribes, that stoppeth his ears from hearing of blood, and shutteth his eyes from seeing evil ..." Isaiah 33:15

This part that I underlined is what got my attention. I realized for the first time in my life that what I look upon and what I listen to will affect my relationship with God. It is very clear that what you feed your mind with will be reflected in your character. If you feed your mind with God's Word, by His grace and the indwelling of the Holy Spirit you will begin to reflect the image of Jesus Christ, but if you feed the mind with the pollution of the world you will reflect a corrupt and worldly character. Truly by beholding you will become changed.

It does not take a rocket scientist to figure out that just about everything that is on TV these days are full of perversion, violence and crime, even the cartoons are filled with violence. So reader, what are you feeding not only your mind, but what are you feeding the minds of your children? That's a pretty sobering question don't you think? The Bible says:

"Love not the world, neither the things [that are] in the world. If any man love the world, the love of the Father is not in him. For all that [is] in the world, the lust of the flesh, and the lust of the eyes, and the pride of life, is not of the Father, but is of the world. And the world passeth away, and the lust thereof: but he that doeth the will of God abideth for ever." I John 2:15–17

So, I ask you this; what in this world could you possible hang onto that will save you in the end? I tell you, nothing. The only hope anybody has is to form a personal relationship with Jesus Christ through His Word.

What most people don't realize is that you can only serve two masters in life, either God or Satan. And the majority of people that may think they are serving God have really been deceived into serving Satan, because they have allowed someone to interpret the Bible for them and not allowed the Bible to interpret itself. Also, many live their lives according to the traditions of men and not according to the Word of God. They pick and choose the Commandments they want to keep so that they can continue to live in sin and directly disobey God's Law, which is unchangeable. For if it were changeable Jesus Christ would not have had to die on the cross for us. Let's think about this for a moment. Don't you think that if God could have changed His Law to make an adjustment for man's sin that God would have chosen this rather than to see His only Son suffer the way He did and be crucified for our sins? This thought in itself should make it clear that the Ten Commandments that God has given in His Word are unchangeable. After all, that is why He wrote it with His own finger on stone. (Please read *Exodus 31:18.*)

Most people just go along with what the preacher is saying as if he or she is perfect. Let me share something with you; reader, all preachers, pastors, priests, and the even the pope are sinful just like everybody else; and not one of them can get you into heaven nor forgive you of your sins. Only Jesus was perfect and can forgive you for your sins. You will be held personally responsible for your relationship with God. So I encourage you, don't listen to what other people say, work out your own salvation with fear and trembling. For in the end you will give account for the light that you have received as well as for the light you had opportunity to receive, but rejected.

Most people reject new light from the Word of God because it is not what their preacher teaches or it is not what they were taught by their families. Let me ask you this, the church that you are going to, do you go there because this is where God has led you through His Word, or is it because your family or a friend goes there; or you like going there because of the music and the people seem to be sincere? I encourage you to evaluate the reason you attend the church you currently attend. Search the Scriptures and ask God to lead you and don't let anybody influence your decision. If you truly love God you will let Him lead you. And if you are not currently going to a church I encourage you as well to search the Scriptures for yourself and let God lead you. For those that put their trust in man to lead them in the right direction will surely enough be led in the wrong direction. For the Bible says:

> *"Thus saith the Lord; Cursed [be] the man that trusteth in man, and maketh flesh his arm, and whose heart departeth from the Lord." Jeremiah 17:5*

So there you have it, a direct warning from God Himself. So who are you going to trust?

After I finished my classes it was time to find a job. I always dreaded filling out the application because it would get to that part that said, "Have you ever been convicted of a felony? If so, please explain." I knew I had to tell the truth for God hates a liar.

> *"These six [things] doth the Lord hate: yea, seven [are] an abomination unto him: A proud look, a lying tongue, and hands that shed innocent blood." Proverbs 6:16, 17*

> *"A false witness shall not be unpunished, and [he that] speaketh lies shall not escape ... A false witness shall not be unpunished, and [he that] speaketh lies shall perish." Proverbs 19:5, 9*

I knew I just had to trust God and He would work things out. I realized in my relationship with the Lord that if I would be faithful to Him and trust Him, He would be faithful to me. Then one day a church member asked me if I had any construction experience, and I told him I had a little. I had gone to school for building trades but never really pursued it as a career. He told me he would start me out at eight dollars an hour. I thought to myself, "It's been twenty years since I made eight dollars an hour." But I had to start somewhere. Then I remembered that it was quite a bit more than I made when I was working in prison where I was only paid twelve cents an hour. This was a very nice raise, praise God! (Besides nobody else wanted to give me a job because my felony was a violent crime against a federal agent.) Not only that, I knew God wanted me to take this job. Nothing else mattered anymore. I was willing to go where God was directing and do whatever He asked. I had to learn how to be content wherever I was in life.

At the homeless shelter, after you start working, you are required to put away seventy five percent of your earnings. Once a month I would sit down with my case manager to go over my savings and my goals. As the months went by I was in need of transportation. My boss had given me his bike to ride back and forth to the shop, and then he would take me to the job site from there. One day, on the way to work I saw an old station wagon for sale, so I checked into it. The owner only wanted six hundred dollars for it. I prayed about it and talked to my case manager. She told me that they don't advise the residents to purchase vehicles while living there. However, she realized that I was a very determined person and that if I was going to continue to work in the construction field I would need a car. My boss helped me out with the purchase and we got it for four hundred and fifty dollars. It was very clean and ran well. Another blessing from God!

Shortly after I starting work I was able to move from the dorm living quarters to the transitional area where two people would share a room. This allowed me to have a lot more quite time to study and pray. During my stay at the shelter

I would spend most of my time praying in the little chapel, witnessing and sharing the gospel truth with others. I would invite people to church and pray with them as well. It was always exciting to share God's Word. I tried to take advantage of every opportunity to pass out Bible studies and books to residents and staff personnel.

One time in a meeting with my case manager, she noticed that I was not meeting my required amount of savings according to the seventy-five percent rule. As she reviewed my outgoing expenses, she noticed that I was giving ten percent of my income to the church and a small offering as well. She started to tell me that she did not think I should be doing this, and that God would understand if I did not pay my tithes. I said to her, "You don't understand, if it was not for God I would not even be alive today." (She went on to explain that I needed to be saving as much as possible and that if I was not applying myself to the requirements that they might have to, "time me out" for seven days.) I then explained to her that according to the Word of God, the Lord requires that all people return ten percent of their earnings to Him; for in doing so you will receive a blessing.

For it is written:

> *"Bring ye all the tithes into the storehouse, that there may be meat in Mine house, and prove Me now herewith, saith the Lord of hosts, if I will not open you the windows of heaven, and pour you out a blessing, that [there shall] not [be room] enough [to receive it]." Malachi 3:10*

I told her that they could do whatever they thought was necessary. Reader, it is better to live in poverty with God's blessing than to live in comfort knowing that you will soon face the judgment of God for openly and willingly breaking the eighth Commandment, "*thou shall not steal*." See also *Malachi 3:6–8.*

I would like to share a quote from one of my favorite authors.

> *"It is man's duty to be faithful in giving the Lord the portion which He claims in tithes and offerings, that there may be a supply to carry forward the work without embarrassment of hindrance is plainly specified. Duty is duty, and should be performed for its own sake. But the Lord has compassion upon us in our fallen condition, and accompanies His commands with promises. He calls upon His people to prove Him, declaring that He will reward obedience with the richest blessings." Sabbath School Worker, Feb. 14, 1905*

I remember the first time I attended church and the offering plate came by; it broke my heart because I thought of all the money I had wasted in the past and now, after all the Lord has done for me, I could not give an offering. It took all I had to hold back the tears. When I was finally able to give an offering and pay my tithes I felt great joy. Well, my caseworker did not time me out and I thank God for helping me be faithful.

Reader, don't ever think that you cannot afford to pay your tithes and give an offering for I tell you the truth when I say, "You can't afford not to." I have personally experienced the blessing that comes from being faithful to God. One of the best blessings of all is a continued deeper experience with God in my life throughout each day.

The Bible says; "*Thou shall not steal*." And all those that disobey God by not paying their tithes are robbing God. They are in direct violation of the eighth Commandment. (See *Exodus 20.16*) The Bible says:

"Will a man rob God? Yet ye have robbed me. But ye say, Wherein have we robbed Thee? In tithes and offerings." Malachi 3:8

The Bible is very plain yet so many feel that their money belongs to them, that they earned it. But who gave you the ability to earn that money? It was God. For it is written:

"But thou shalt remember the LORD thy God: for [it is] He that giveth thee power to get wealth." Deuteronomy 8:18

Many people feel that they have the right to indulge in whatever they please. That all they have they have earned by their own hands. They feel as if they have built their house with their power and their might. I encourage you to read the story in the Bible the Book of *Daniel chapter 4,* pay close attention to *verses 30, 31* and what follows as a result of one thinking in this manner.

Another quote from a favorite author:

"So many are constantly giving up their tithes and offerings to worldly living, to self-indulgence in the lust of the flesh. Those that selfishly withhold their means need not be surprised if God's hand scatters their possessions. That which should have been devoted to the advancement of His work and cause, but which has been withheld, may in various ways be taken away. God will come near to them in judgments. Many losses will be sustained. God can scatter the means He has lent to His stewards, if they refuse to use it to His glory." Sabbath School Worker, Feb. 21, 1905

—Twenty-two—
Moving Out of the Homeless Shelter

I had been at the shelter for almost one year now and was able to save up enough money to move out. Again the Lord had made a way for me. One of the church members had a daughter that wanted to sell her house. He offered it to me on a land contract. I received the house for several thousands of dollars under the actual value of the home, which made it possible for me to have a low monthly house payment. Again, what a blessing from God! The Lord was teaching me how to be content in life and I was beginning to look at things much differently now. It did not matter to me if I did not have the things that I once possessed. What I had now was sufficient for my needs. I also realized that God does not want His children to get attached to this world for we are just passing through.

Now I had a new life, I had been born again. I continued to study God's word and share with others. During my stay at the shelter, I was praying; earnestly seeking God's will. I had been writing poems and reflections from Scripture and I felt as if the Lord was leading me to write a book. It had been a couple days since I made a direct petition to God in regards to this. I asked Him to show me in a way that I would be 100% sure. I wanted to be sure as I did not want to waste time doing something the Lord did not want me to do.

One evening I was strongly impressed by the Holy Spirit to read a passage out of the Bible. I heard the soft-spoken voice say, "Read *Jeremiah 30:2*." At first I thought nothing of it, so I continued on with my devotions that evening and went to bed. The next morning I got up, prayed, and began my morning devotions. Again the soft spoken voice said to me, "Read *Jeremiah 30:2*." I thought maybe I was just talking to myself but to be sure, I turned to the passage, and as before God gave me clear direction. During my prayer I asked the Lord to show me in a way that there would be no doubt in my mind as to whether He wanted me to write a book. The passage reads:

> *"Thus speaketh the* L*ORD God of Israel, saying, Write thee all the words that I have spoken unto thee in a book."*

I had my answer. It took me about a year to begin and I struggled as to where to start. The Lord had shown me many things in the Scriptures. One day it came to me ... it starts with your testimony!

During this year I had written the people from the *Amazing Facts* Bible School in Indiana, and asked if I could meet with them. I had been corresponding with them for almost two and half years now and I wanted to thank them personally for their devotion to prison ministry. They made arrangements for me to meet them at a church that was about halfway for both of us and also made it possible for me to share my testimony. They are very loving and devoted people to God's work. I rejoiced in the opportunity to share my conversion experience and my walk with God. After I had given my testimony the group rejoiced and praised God. At that time they asked me if I did sermons, too. Without thinking too much, I told them "yes." I figured God would give me the words to speak if I asked Him. At a later date I went back and shared all that the Lord revealed to me through prayer and searching the Scriptures.

After this one of the people in the group invited me to speak at another church in Centerville, Michigan. On the way home from work one Sunday I was thinking of this upcoming appointment and about what I should pray for. I wanted to pray that I would be given the sermon time so that

I could share my testimony and do a brief sermon that tied in with my testimony at the same time. The few times I was able to share my testimony I did it during Sabbath School time (a study time just before the sermon) and not everyone was able to hear.

When I arrived home within a half hour I got a phone call from the pastor of the Centerville church wanting to confirm that I was coming on the scheduled date. He then went on to tell me that they were expecting to hear my testimony and a sermon, during the sermon time. Wow! I did not even get my prayer out to God regarding this; I was only thinking about what I would like to ask for. I remembered a passage in the Bible that says:

"And it shall come to pass, that before they call, I will answer; and while they are yet speaking, I will hear." Isaiah 65:24

God is so good!—on my way to that church I was praying first for God to help me speak because I was always nervous in front of people. I also asked God that if this was what He wanted me to do; I wanted Him to put it on the hearts of the people or the pastors to invite me to future appointments. That way I would know that God was going before me and preparing the way. Upon my arrival, as soon as I walked in the door, a woman that I had not yet met from the *Amazing Facts* Bible School handed me her pastor's card and told me that he would like me to come and speak at two of his churches. Then, after the service, another gentleman approached me and asked me if I would come out to Pennsylvania and speak at two of his churches. Again I was in awe of God's guidance in my life.

By the end of the year I had spoken at about twenty places, including Andrews University to some of the seminary students; and to finish off the year I had given my testimony to two small groups of Amish people and did a week of prison ministry. Here I was able to witness to inmates at county jails, and was even able to speak at one of the state prisons with other people like myself who had been delivered by God from a very corrupt lifestyle, as well as with others that had not excepted Jesus Christ as their Saviour and Lord of their lives. We would encourage inmates to take advantage of the time they had in lock down to form a personal relationship with Jesus Christ, our Lord and Saviour. What joy there is in serving the Lord. As a result of our week of prison ministry we had about one hundred seventy five to two hundred inmates sign up for the *Amazing Facts* Bible studies. We were invited also to come back to the state prison to do Bible studies or sermons one day a month for the next year. What a blessing!

Just to show you that all things are possible with God, I would like to share this with you. Regarding my speaking at the state prison, I was required to fill out a criminal history report. I had answered all question and told them that I was still on probation with the federal government and explained my case. You see the federal and state law states that no one is permitted to visit or volunteer for services in a state or federal prison for up to two years after being off probation. Yet, there I was inside speaking to a large group of state prisoners. I even told them with God there is no wall or obstacle that God is unable to get through; because I was standing there speaking to them I was a testimony to this. I once read a sign at our church that said, "When God points the way His hand has already made it possible." When you take one step He has already taken two.

I would like to say, Jesus has His hand of love stretched out to you and longs to comfort you. Where else could one go? It is the words of Jesus that comforts the soul. Where could we ever find a love like His—so devoted, sincere, pure, holy and true, so full of grace, too. His love is truly demonstrated at the cross, and it is at the cross our new life begins. Please, my friend, don't walk away from the love of Jesus that will set you free. This world has nothing to offer but torment, emptiness, and despair. I plead with you to give Jesus a chance. He is offering to you a free gift of salvation, an invitation for eternal life. Just take it one day at a time, pray and spend time in the Word of God and He will give you strength, courage, and lift you up in a special way. Just keep your eyes on Jesus for He is coming soon!

—TWENTY-THREE—
My Closing Thoughts

In closing, I would like to share this with you. I, without knowing it, served Satan just about my whole life. Sure at first it seemed to be fun. I had power, money, and pleasure. Where did it get me in the end? I reaped emptiness, loneliness, bitterness, resentment, and eventually hatred and close to death. I tell you the truth if you have not figured this out yet. The end results of serving the enemy of God Almighty are the things I just listed above and more. If you will but invite the Holy One in, Jesus Christ the Lamb of God, He will show you a way that will bless your life completely.

> *"But as it is written, Eye hath not seen, nor ear heard, neither have entered into the heart of man, the things which God hath prepared for them that love Him." I Corinthians 2:9*

> *"Many are inquiring, "How am I to make the surrender of myself to God?" You desire to give yourself to Him, but you are weak in moral power, in slavery to doubt, and controlled by the habits of your life of sin. Your promises and resolutions are like ropes of sand. You cannot control your thoughts, your impulses, your affections. The knowledge of your broken promises and forfeited pledges weakens your confidence in your own sincerity, and causes you to feel that God cannot accept you; but you need not despair. What you need to understand is the true force of the will. This is the governing power in the nature of man, the power of decision, or of choice. Everything depends on the right action of the will. The power of choice God has given to men; it is*

theirs to exercise. You cannot change your heart, you cannot of yourself give to God its affections; but you can choose to serve Him. You can give Him your will; He will then work in you to will and to do according to His good pleasure. Thus your whole nature will be brought under the control of the Spirit of Christ; your affections will be centered upon Him, your thoughts will be in harmony with Him." Steps to Christ, pg. 47

"That He would grant you, according to the riches of His glory, to be strengthened with might by His Spirit in the inner man; That Christ may dwell in your hearts by faith; that ye, being rooted and grounded in love, May be able to comprehend with all saints what [is] the breadth, and length, and depth, and height; And to know the love of Christ, which passeth knowledge, that ye might be filled with all the fulness of God. <u>Now unto Him that is able to do exceeding abundantly above all that we ask or think</u>, according to the power that worketh in us, Unto Him [be] glory in the church by Christ Jesus throughout all ages, world without end. Amen." Ephesians 3:16–21

Here is a quote by an author named, Jean Handwerk:

"Speaking the Gospel truth will anger some, but would you rather face their anger of God's rejection of you for failing to speak it for others salvation. Speaking the Gospel truth will cause some to speak ill of our church—but how many more will seek us out because we do tell it? Speaking the Gospel truth may cost you many of your friends—but they will be replaced with others—whose value and goals are more aligned with yours. Speaking the Gospel truth may separate you from your family—but would you do them any eternal good by rejecting

your faith in order to earn their acceptance? Speaking the Gospel truth will attract criticism and ridicule to yourself—but it will also attract God's grace and the power of the Holy Spirit."

So I ask, will you make a stand for Jesus and speak the truth? There is nothing we can do to add to the beauty of the Gospel truth; may we speak it as it reads and allow the Holy Spirit to do the rest.

My friend, if there is anything that you take out of this whole book, I plead with you, take this. The enemy's biggest fear is that we call upon the shed blood of Jesus to cleanse and cover us; and that we take God at His word and believe that He will do what He has said and promised.

In the following pages, I would like to share with you some poems that the Lord has inspired me to write. Along with some of these are reflections from Scripture, other authors, and personal thoughts. May God bless you as you read them and reflect.

The Love of Jesus

Even when we forsake Him, His love is still there.
He just bows His head and sheds another tear.
His love will never fade away or bend, it will always remain strong my friend.
If you choose to accept His love it will never leave, so my friend please believe.
His blood has been cleansing us of our sins over the years.
And it is His love that will continue to comfort us in our times of fear. His love will forever flow, solid as a rock and enriched with a heavenly glow.

One can understand a love like His, so faithful, rich in mercy and full of compassion, this is the love that He gives.
His love remains strong hour after hour, it will never fade away like a withering flower.
So my friend, don't embrace the things of this world, things that are given to sway and fade away.
Embrace the everlasting and don't go astray.
Enjoy the love, joy, and peace of Jesus Christ that will never cease. This is the love that He shares for you and I, it will never change nor ever die.

I encourage you to seek the Lord with all you heart, mind, body and all your strength, for trying times are upon us and Jesus Christ is the only way. Search the Scriptures for yourself.

> *"Prove all things; hold fast that which is good. Abstain from all appearance of evil." I Thessalonians 5:21, 22*

> *"Study to show thyself approved unto God, a workman that needeth not to be ashamed, rightly dividing the word of truth." II Timothy 2:15*

Put not your trust in flesh, for in doing so you are setting yourself up for a snare. Satan is very crafty and will always mix lies with the truth as he did when tempting Eve in the garden.

The days are at hand that there will be great turmoil in this country and the people will blame God's true church and will seek to utterly destroy them; but God will seal and protect a remnant that will go forth with power that will be unmatched, for this will be those that will be filled with the outpouring of the true Holy Spirit and none will be able to withstand them. Consider what I say, and may the Lord Jesus Christ give you understanding in all things.

The Love of God

My love for you is like the rain pouring down to this world.
Like the melting ice in the polar caps dripping with tears.
Like the early morning dew.
It's Continuous.

My love for you is like the ocean waves crashing on the shores.
Like the wind in the trees and the birds singing their sweet melodies.
It's Never-ending.

My love for you is like the stars in the night sky.
Like darkness to space and light to the sun.
It's Everlasting.

My love for you is like a puzzle that can never be pieced together. As one can not search the depths of the ocean and seas, it remains a mystery.
It's Un-searchable.

Just know My love is always with you like the lilies in the fields and the sweet aroma to a rose.
It's Forever.

When I first wrote this poem I wrote it for someone that I loved very much. But as I started to understand and know the Lord Jesus Christ I began to realize that He inspired me to write this to share His love for me and you. As I continued to learn more about God I also realized that I could never love anyone to this depth without His love dwelling in me, for I could only love another as I learn and accept the love of Jesus Christ.

Thy Word is My Delight

My Lord, may Thy Spirit convict me strongly of anything that I may do or say that is not in harmony with Thy will today.
As Thou are the true Vine Oh, Lord;
It is my desire to abide in Thee, that Thou may work through me to produce fruit abundantly.
I delight in Thy law Oh, Lord, as it is perfect restoring my soul.
Thy statutes bring rejoicing to my heart as I feel Thy Holy Spirit flow.
For the Commandment of the Lord is pure, enlightening my eyes and filling me up with a heavenly glow.
The love of the Lord endures forever and Thy judgments are truly righteous altogether.
For in Thy word Oh, Lord am I warned and by keeping them I am reborn.

Surrender

Teach me, Oh Lord, the way of Thy statutes.
Give me understanding and I shall keep Thy law.
Incline my heart unto Thy testimonies and not to covetousness.
Establish Thy word unto Thy servant who is devoted to Thy fear.

For I have hoped in Thy judgments and mercies.
Catch me when I fall, give me strength and courage to fulfill the purpose in which I was called.
Open Thou mine eyes, that I may behold wondrous things out of Thy law.
Thou, Oh Lord, are my Mighty Redeemer, for Thou has purchased me with Thy blood. In Thee will I trust, and to Thee do I surrender all.

To My Heavenly Father

I have but one life to give and I give it unto Thee. I have not words to express my thanksgiving; therefore I will do my best to reflect this in word and deed. Thou has said, "If ye love Me keep My commandments." For this shall I do, and with Thy grace only shall I come through. I will need every bit of strength that Thou are willing to give that I may remain dependent up Thee. Calling upon the shed blood of Thy Son to keep me clean and free from the sins that have stained my heart within. Crying out for a clean heart within. For it is His robe of righteousness that I desire to wear, for my righteousness is filthy and this garment I do not wish to share. I seek to be cleansed from secret faults. Keep back Thy servant also from presumptuous sins; let them not have dominion over me: then shall I be upright, and I shall be innocent from the great transgression.

I will call upon Thy Holy Spirit to keep my mind upon Jesus and away from thoughts of sin. For Thy embracement is more precious than silver and gold. For it is Thee that I rejoice to embrace, the Ancient of Days for this is my goal. It is my desire to praise Thee in the midst of the congregations and speak of Thy mighty works, for they are uncountable like the grains of sand upon the sea. For Thou, Father, are justified in all the judgments and perfect in all Thy ways. Thou are truly worthy of all blessings and praise. Thou are so full of compassion and so very kind, Thou has not only been a Father to me, but also a friend of mine. Now unto the King eternal, immortal, be honor and glory forever and ever. Amen

—Twenty-four—
As Words Flow Through Me to You

Let no doubt arise among us as to whether or not the Lord knows what is going on in our lives, for His Holy Word says:

"... I will never leave thee, nor forsake thee." Hebrews 13:5

Therefore, let us remember it is written that it is:

"... impossible for God to lie." Hebrews 6:18

He has said "*I will never leave thee*," therefore He is always with us. So as the raging storm of evil increases, with chaos growing at an alarming rate, the Lord of Hosts is with us.

"Lo, I am with you alway, [even] unto the end of the world." Matthew 28:20

The Lord is very well aware of our sufferings. There is no thought or sorrow that is within that we could possibly keep from God.

"... Thou, [even] Thou only, knowest the hearts of all the children of men." I Kings 8:39

The Lord knows the pain of loneliness and grief that lies within our hearts, the hopelessness that we feel due to the overwhelming influences of evil that surrounds us daily, concerns for our children and loved ones, the doubts we have and the fear that we hide within. For we truly stand naked before the Lord.

> *"All things [are] naked and opened unto the eyes of Him with whom we have to do." Hebrews 4:13*

Our hearts are laid bare to the divine eye of Jesus. There is no disease, sickness, or weakness that our Saviour is not able to feel, for He is touched with our infirmities (*Hebrews 4:15*). My friends, we are living in a world of suffering, difficulty, trial, and sorrow. All this awaits us along the way to the heavenly home. God never said that it was going to be easy; but He bids all that are weary and oppressed:

> *"Come unto Me, all [ye] that labour and are heavy laden, and I will give you rest. Take My yoke upon you, and learn of Me; for I am meek and lowly in heart: and ye shall find rest unto your souls. For My yoke [is] easy, and My burden is light." Matthew 11:28–30*

Let us not make life's burdens doubly heavy by continually anticipating trouble or by hanging onto emotional pain, for these things will only bring one deeper into despair. Satan's desire is for us to feel that we cannot approach God to ask Him for comfort because we are unworthy sinful people; but I tell you, our Saviour Jesus Christ longs to help us overcome and to heal us from our infirmities within.

> *"Let us therefore come boldly unto the throne of grace that we may obtain mercy, and find grace to help in time of need." Hebrews 4:16*

> *"Casting all your care upon Him; for He careth for you." I Peter 5:7*

Therefore, bring every heartache, fear, doubt, worry and any other pain that is causing separation between you and God, to the throne of grace that you may obtain divine influence and courage to overcome. Let not the enemy keep your mind diverted from Jesus our Redeemer for another moment.

> *"God [is] our refuge and strength, a very present help in trouble." Psalms 46:1*

> *"Cast thy burden upon the Lord, and He shall sustain thee." Psalms 55:22*

Prayer is the answer to every problem we face. It puts us in tune with divine wisdom which knows how to adjust everything perfectly. So often we do not pray in certain situations, because from our standpoint, the outlook is hopeless; but, nothing is impossible with God (*Luke 1:37*). Nothing is too entangled that it cannot be remedied. No human relationship is too strained for God to bring about reconciliation and understanding. No habit so deep rooted that it cannot be overcome:

> *"No one is so weak that he cannot be strong. No one is so ill that he cannot be healed. No mind is so dull that it cannot be made brilliant. Whatever we need, if we trust God, He will supply it. If anything is causing worry and anxiety, let us stop rehearsing the difficulty and trust God for healing, love, and power." Review and Herald Oct. 7, 1865*

The world is not going to get any better but only worse. I say this, not to discourage you, but to encourage you to form a deep personal relationship with Jesus Christ. He will walk with you every moment of the day as well as in the most difficult times of your life. When you feel that you can go no further close your eyes and focus on the cross in which our Saviour endured for us.

"Draw nigh to God, and He will draw nigh to you." James 4:8

"I can do all things through Christ which strengtheneth me." Philippians 4:13

"For God hath not given us the spirit of fear; but of power, and of love, and of a sound mind." II Timothy 1:7

Let not our hearts grow weary and faint but let us grab onto the Word of God in faith holding fast to the promises He has made. Remember:

"...Without faith [it is] impossible to please [Him]: for he that cometh to God must believe that He is, and [that] He is a rewarder of them that diligently seek Him." Hebrews 11:6

The key words here are <u>faith</u>, <u>believe</u>, and <u>diligent</u>.

"Being confident of this very thing, that He which hath begun a good work in you will perform [it] until the day of Jesus Christ." Philippians 1:6

"God hath dealt to every man the measure of faith." Romans 12:3

The Lord has also said:

"I will put My laws into their mind, and write them in their hearts: and I will be to them a God, and they shall be to Me a people." Hebrews 8:10

Believe the words that God has spoken to us through His Holy Word. Jesus said:

"The words that I speak unto you, [they] are spirit, and [they] are life." John 6:63

"All scripture [is] given by inspiration of God, and [is] profitable for doctrine, for reproof, for correction, for instruction in righteousness." II Timothy 3:16

Be diligent in your search to know our Father and Creator of our lives through Christ Jesus, the Word.

"Looking unto Jesus the author and finisher of [our] faith ... He is a rewarder of them that diligently seek Him." Hebrews 12:2; 11:6

The Lord is calling to us:

"My son, (My daughter) give Me thine heart, and let thine eyes observe My ways." Proverbs 23:26

"That He would grant you, according to the riches of His glory, to be strengthened with might by His Spirit in the inner man ... And to know the love of Christ, which passeth knowledge, that ye might be filled with all the fulness of God." Ephesians 3:16, 19

"Acquaint now thyself with Him, and be at peace: thereby good shall come unto thee. Receive, I pray thee, the law from His mouth, and lay up His words in thine heart." Job 22:21, 22

How true is the Word of God! If you would only believe as you read what peace would come upon you and how free you could be from the doubt and fear the enemy continuously impresses upon you. Jesus said:

"And ye shall know the truth, and the truth shall make you free." John 8:32

Our only hope is in Jesus, if you lack faith ask the Lord Who is willing to bestow upon you the increase that is needed to sustain you through the trials you face daily; but remember, as you come to God you must believe that He is. If you lack belief ask the Lord to help your unbelief. The God we serve is so full of love that He is willing to help us with every aspect of our relationship with Him. From our unbelief, lack of faith, and discouragements that fill our hearts due to our lack of understanding; God is even willing to help us be willing if we would just ask. When we get tired of trying to do everything ourselves, may we surrender all to our loving Father and Saviour Jesus Christ.

It truly will be faith that will see us through. Our faith, in knowing Jesus is with us every step of the way. If our spiritual eyes were to be opened we would see the angels the Lord has commanded to stand by our side that hold back the waves of darkness that seek to consume us, but we, too, have a part to fulfill and that is obeying the word of God by depending upon the Father, trusting that He will provide everything we are in need of. May our desire be to count all things but loss for the excellency of the knowledge of Christ Jesus our Lord, that we may know Him, and the power of His resurrection, and the fellowship of His sufferings.

It is clear that we are living in the end times. Our faith will be tested, trials will befall us. God will prove all those that profess to be His followers. God will see who is loyal and faithful to Him and who will choose to embrace the world and the things thereof.

"I the LORD search the heart, [I] try the reins ... I will melt them ... and will try them as gold is tried." Jeremiah 17:10; 9:7; Zechariah 13:9

But God tells us:

"Beloved, think it not strange concerning the fiery trial which is to try you, as though some strange thing happened unto you. But rejoice, inasmuch as ye are partakers of Christ's sufferings." I Peter 4:12, 13

As we are tried in the furnace of affliction it is here where our character is developed. It is here where God molds us for a special work. So let us keep in mind the fact that we are called upon to endure such trials is proof that our loving Saviour sees something in us that is very precious, which He desires to develop.

"For our light affliction, which is but for a moment, worketh for us a far more exceeding [and] eternal weight of glory." II Corinthians 4:17

The test of our faith and patience should be cheerfully accepted rather than dreaded. I know that this may be a hard thing to understand, but as I look back upon all the times my patience was being tried and my faith being tested, I praise God. During these times the Lord opened my eyes to the defectiveness of my character and the things that I was in need of to surrendering to Him. The Lord does this out of love for our eternal happiness. The Lord's will is to restore not destroy:

"For this is the will of God, [even] your sanctification." I Thessalonians 4:3

When trials arise that seem unexplained, however unjustly we may be treated or wrongfully persecuted, let us hold our peace having confidence in God and His Word. Let us seek counsel from God through prayer asking for wisdom, knowledge, and understanding. Let us search for wisdom as if it were hidden treasure. Let us invite the Lord into our hearts to search us out and reveal to us if there be any evil thing in us that we may seek repentance and grace to overcome. Let us seek the passage to the narrow gate knowing the path will be tough but the end thereof is eternal life.

> *"If ye be reproached for the name of Christ, happy [are ye]; for the spirit of glory and of God resteth upon you: on their part He is evil spoken of, but on your part He is glorified ... Yet if [any man suffer] as a Christian, let him not be ashamed; but let him glorify God on this behalf ... Wherefore let them that suffer according to the will of God commit the keeping of their souls [to him] in well doing, as unto a faithful Creator." I Peter 4:14, 16, 19*

> *"For this [is] thankworthy, if a man for conscience toward God endure grief, suffering wrongfully. For what glory [is it], if, when ye be buffeted for your faults, ye shall take it patiently? but if, when ye do well, and suffer [for it], ye take it patiently, this [is] acceptable with God. For even hereunto were ye called: because Christ also suffered for us, leaving us an example, that ye should follow His steps." I Peter 2:19–21*

Let us not shame ourselves by indulging in a spirit of retaliation and allowing the enemy to rob us of our peace for this will only show that we have not faith and confidence in God to sustain us through these times. The enemy's desire is to captivate our minds with fear and doubt as well as to stir our hearts to murmur and complain. Satan will also desire to fill our hearts with pride, impressing upon us to make a stand through force; as he will whisper in your ear that you are weak and helpless if you do not fight back. Satan will encourage you to put your trust in flesh and not in God. Therefore it is written for our warning:

> *"Cursed [be] the man that trusteth in man, and maketh flesh his arm, and whose heart departeth from the Lord." Jeremiah 17:5*

> *"Those that forget how utterly dependent they are upon God and regard themselves as wise and independent, those that forsake the Mighty One, the source of all strength, and affiliate with the men of the world, placing on them their dependence only become weak in moral power, as are those in whom they trust. All whose heart departeth from the Lord will only open the way for evil influences to make there way in and bring them to ruin." Review and Herald Aug. 4, 1904*

May our prayer be, "Oh, God of mercy and grace, may it be known that I am weak, and in need of Thy counsel, and strength. Therefore, I call upon Thy Holy Name. For if I look to man for strength I will only be weakened. Or to trust in man I shall be deceived, and to seek counsel in flesh will only bring me to ruin. I lift up my voice to Thee my Father and praise Thy greatness for there is no other God but Thee, for Thou sustains me with Thy breath, and comforts me with Thy Spirit of peace. Thou counsels me through Thy Word of truth. I will give my praise and honor to no other, for Thou are the only true Living God; therefore, I will hold fast to Thy promises."

> *"No weapon that is formed against thee shall prosper; and every tongue that] shall rise against thee in judgment thou shalt condemn. This [is] the heritage of the servants of the Lord, and their righteousness [is] of Me, saith the Lord." Isaiah 54:17*

> *"The Lord knoweth how to deliver the godly out of temptations, and to reserve the unjust unto the Day of Judgment to be punished." II Peter 2:9*

> *"That the trial of your faith, being much more precious than of gold that perisheth, though it be tried with fire, might be found unto praise and honour and glory at the appearing of Jesus Christ." I Peter 1:7*

> *"For whatsoever things were written aforetime were written for our learning, that we through patience and comfort of the scriptures might have hope." Romans 15:4*

> *"Trust in the LORD with all thine heart; and lean not unto thine own understanding. In all thy ways acknowledge Him, and He shall direct thy paths." Proverbs 3:5, 6*

Let us seek the Lord with all our hearts, minds, and strength. Let us cry out for conviction that we may know the sin that lies deep in the heart, that we may bring fruit worthy of repentance. May the Lord alert our minds and stir our hearts to make a diligent search that we may know all that would keep us out of the Kingdom of Heaven.

> *"And that, knowing the time, that now [it is] high time to awake out of sleep: for now [is] our salvation nearer than when we believed. The night is far spent, the day is at hand: let us therefore cast off the works of darkness, and let us put on the armour of light." Romans 13:11, 12*

Let us not be foolish to await a great crises before we search out to know the Lord, for the longer we walk in darkness embracing the things of this world, the thicker the miry clay becomes around our feet; and the deeper we will go into spiritual captivity.

> *"I beseech you therefore, brethren, by the mercies of God, that ye present your bodies a living sacrifice, holy, acceptable unto God, [which is] your reasonable service. And be not conformed to this world: but be ye transformed by the renewing of your mind, that ye may prove what [is] that good, and acceptable, and perfect, will of God." Romans 12:1, 2*

Jesus says:

> *"Yet a little while is the light with you. Walk while ye have the light, lest darkness come upon you: for he that walketh in darkness knoweth not whither he goeth. While ye have light, believe in the light, that ye may be the children of light." John 12:35, 36*

The Bible makes it clear to us that we are living in the last days.

> *"In the last days perilous times shall come. For men shall be lovers of their own selves, covetous, boasters, proud, blasphemers, disobedient to parents, unthankful, unholy, Without natural affection, trucebreakers, false accusers, incontinent, fierce, despisers of those that are good, Traitors, heady, highminded, lovers of pleasures more than lovers of God; Having a form of godliness, but denying the power thereof: from such turn away." II Timothy 3:1–5*

Satan is at work to divert our minds from eternal realities. The enemy seeks to consume our time with instruments of amusement, such as television, video games, worldly books and magazines; along with many other worldly activities. The enemy is even in our churches causing division among God's professed people, bringing about gossip, bitterness, resentment, jealousy, and causing one another to hold grudges and become hateful. The devil is:

"... as a roaring lion, walketh about, seeking whom he may devour." I Peter 5:8

The enemy comes to rob, break down and destroy and he will use every person that yields to his temptation to do his dirty work.

The enemy's mouth is full of deceit and oppression: under his tongue is mischief and vanity. Reader, are you letting the enemy use you to do his dirty work? Please give heed to the convictions of the Holy Spirit and grieve not the Spirit. Turn to God and invite Him into your heart to search you out to see if there be any evil thing in you, and to lead you in the way of everlasting. Then ask God to forgive you and create in you a clean heart and renew a right spirit within you. Hold onto Jesus and His words for they are our only hope in life!

Let us accept the victory that Jesus gave us at the cross, as He was the sacrifice for all the sins of mankind. It is at the cross Jesus demonstrated to the world LOVE THROUGH OBEDIENCE CONQUERS ALL.

"Let this mind be in you, which was also in Christ Jesus: Who, being in the form of God, thought it not robbery to be equal with God: But made Himself of no reputation, and took upon Him the form of a servant, and was made in the likeness of men: And being found in fashion as a man, He humbled Himself, and became obedient unto death, even the death of the cross." Philippians 2:5–8

Wow! What love, what compassion, what humility, may we accept the grace that our heavenly Father offers that we may follow the example that His only Son, Jesus Christ, has given.

> *"Let no corrupt communication proceed out of your mouth, but that which is good to the use of edifying, that it may minister grace unto the hearers. And grieve not the Holy Spirit of God, whereby ye are sealed unto the day of redemption. Let all bitterness, and wrath, and anger, and clamour, and evil speaking, be put away from you, with all malice: And be ye kind one to another, tenderhearted, forgiving one another, even as God for Christ's sake hath forgiven you." Ephesians 4:29–32*

> *"Thus speaketh the LORD of hosts, saying, Execute true judgment, and show mercy and compassions every man to his brother: And oppress not the widow, nor the fatherless, the stranger, nor the poor; and let none of you imagine evil against his brother in your heart." Zechariah 7:9, 10*

Oh, how we should love one another, what a difference it would make not only in our lives but in the lives of others. With anger comes bitterness, resentment and hate. All these things do nothing but absorb thoughts and bring about stress which brings about ill health. The end result is destruction to one's own life. Jesus tells us that we should love one another as He has loved us (*John 15:12*). Reader, please don't let your life be eaten away with resentment, bitterness and hatred. Life is too short and there is much joy to be gained by love. It is written:

> *"Be not deceived; God is not mocked: for whatsoever a man soweth, that shall he also reap. For he that soweth*

to his flesh shall of the flesh reap corruption; but he that soweth to the Spirit shall of the Spirit reap life everlasting. And let us not be weary in well doing: for in due season we shall reap, if we faint not." Galatians 6:7–9

Let the words that we speak be done with compassion and love that others may see and hear the character of Jesus Christ in us. But in order to do this, one must study the life of Jesus. Take note of how He spoke to people, with gentleness and compassion. He did not condemn nor speak harsh tones that would discourage someone from coming to Him. His character was humble and peaceful even unto the death of the cross. He even prayed for those that crucified Him, saying:

"Father, forgive them; for they know not what they do." Luke 23:34

My friend, when was the last time that you prayed for the person that caused you pain, whether it was emotional or physical? Could you pray to the Father and ask Him to forgive that person, or persons, for what they have done because they do not understand how the enemy has used them to do his evil deeds. I encourage you, my friend, to do this as well as ask God to help you forgive them. Let not the enemy snare you by causing you to harbor any type of bitterness towards fellow human beings. Jesus said:

"For if ye forgive men their trespasses, your heavenly Father will also forgive you: But if ye forgive not men their trespasses, neither will your Father forgive your trespasses." Matthew 6:14, 15

My friend, God does not forgive on condition, so neither should we. And, yes, God will help you to forgive if you ask Him for the help.

> *"Charity (or love) suffereth long, [and] is kind; charity envieth not; charity vaunteth not itself, is not puffed up, Doth not behave itself unseemly, seeketh not her own, is not easily provoked, thinketh no evil; Rejoiceth not in iniquity, but rejoiceth in the truth; Beareth all things, believeth all things, hopeth all things, endureth all things. Charity never faileth." I Corinthians 13:4–8*

> *"Love worketh no ill to his neighbour: therefore love [is] the fulfilling of the law." Romans 13:10*

How is your love today? My friend, I encourage you to read through this verse and put your name in front of each phrase. For example if your name is John say this; John's love suffereth long, John is kind, John's love envieth not and so on until you have read through all verses here. Then listen to the Holy Spirit speak to your heart and give heed to the conviction that comes to the places where you fall short. Write them down and ask God to forgive you and strengthen you in these areas. I say write them down so that you won't forget the very topic that you need help with. What blessings to your life and to those around you will come when you do this. And, my friend, it would be beneficial if we all did this often.

Let us all carefully read *Matthew 25:31–46*, and may we lay these words to heart.

> *"Finally, brethren, whatsoever things are true, whatsoever things [are] honest, whatsoever things [are] just, whatsoever things [are] pure, whatsoever things [are] lovely, whatsoever things [are] of good report; if [there*

be] any virtue, and if [there be] any praise, think on these things." Philippians 4:8

Remember:

"God shall supply all your need according to his riches in glory by Christ Jesus." Philippians 4:19

—Twenty-Five—
The Second Coming of Christ

Reader, please give these Bible verses some very serious thought. Let not your mind be deceived for Jesus is coming and the Bible makes it very clear as to how this will take place. These are very important questions that we need to know because Satan will try to impersonate and counterfeit the second coming of Jesus Christ. Satan will appear as an angel of light and will deceive nearly the whole world. The Bible tells us:

"And no marvel; for Satan himself is transformed into an angel of light." II Corinthians 11:14

The Apostle Paul goes on to tell us:

"But though we, or an angel from heaven, preach any other gospel unto you than that which we have preached unto you, let him be accursed." Galatians 1:8

The Bible tells us:

"Christ was once offered to bear the sins of many; and unto them that look for Him shall he appear the second time without sin unto salvation." Hebrews 9:28

So here we see a promise that Jesus Christ will come again. Jesus goes on to tell us:

"Let not your heart be troubled: ye believe in God, believe also in Me. In My Father's house are many mansions: if [it were] not [so], I would have told you. I go to

prepare a place for you. And if I go and prepare a place for you, I will come again, and receive you unto Myself; that where I am, [there] ye may be also." John 14:1–3

What a blessing to know this. Jesus is coming back to gather those that belong to Him and take them to a mansion that He has prepared for them. Wow! So many people today waste so much precious time trying to build a mansion here in this world that they don't get to know Jesus Christ, our Saviour, and don't know that He has prepared a place that goes beyond our imagination. What a precious gift!

Reader, don't miss out, nothing in this world compares to this! Please don't let yourself get so caught up in this world that you don't take the time to get to know Jesus.

So how will Jesus come the second time?

"And when He had spoken these things, while they beheld, He was taken up; and a cloud received Him out of their sight. And while they looked stedfastly toward heaven as He went up, behold, two men stood by them in white apparel; Which also said, Ye men of Galilee, why stand ye gazing up into heaven? this same Jesus, which is taken up from you into heaven, shall so come in like manner as ye have seen Him go into heaven." Acts 1:9–11

This passage makes it clear that Jesus Christ will return coming from heaven.

So what will it be like?

"For as the lightning cometh out of the east, and shineth even unto the west; so shall also the coming of the Son of man be." Matthew 24:27

"Behold, He cometh with clouds; and every eye shall see Him, and they [also] which pierced Him: and all kindreds of the earth shall wail because of Him." Revelation 1:7

The Bible is clear, Jesus will appear in the clouds and every eye shall see Him. And this does not mean on TV. Reader, if you are seeing some television broadcast in regards to Jesus Christ being somewhere in the world it is a lie. The Bible is very clear when it says every eye shall see Him (Jesus Christ). Now you may be thinking, "How will everyone in the world see Jesus Christ coming at the same time." Let us leave that up to God, after all He does hold the whole universe in place and calls every star by its name. (See *Psalms 147:4*) So you will not need anybody to tell you, as the event will be so grand that there will be no mistaking the event if you have studied the Bible and believe what it says.

Remember what Jesus said:

"Then if any man shall say unto you, Lo, here [is] Christ, or there; believe [it] not. For there shall arise false Christs, and false prophets, and shall show great signs and wonders; insomuch that, if [it were] possible, they shall deceive the very elect. Behold, I have told you before. Wherefore if they shall say unto you, Behold, He is in the desert; go not forth: behold, [He is] in the secret chambers; believe [it] not." Matthew 24:23–26

"And they shall say to you, See here; or, see there: go not after [them], nor follow [them]. For as the lightning, that lighteneth out of the one [part] under heaven, shineth unto the other [part] under heaven; so shall also the Son of man be in His day." Luke 17:23, 24

What else will be happening?

> *"And the heaven departed as a scroll when it is rolled together; and every mountain and island were moved out of their places." Revelation 6:14*

> *"But the day of the Lord will come as a thief in the night; in the which the heavens shall pass away with a great noise, and the elements shall melt with fervent heat, the earth also and the works that are therein shall be burned up." II Peter 3:10*

Wow! This will be no quiet event for the heavens shall depart and pass away with a great noise. Mountains and islands will be moved out of their places and people will be fleeing for their lives in fear of the wrath of God. The Bible says:

> *"For the great day of His wrath is come; and who shall be able to stand?" Revelation 6:17*

Reader, knowing this, what could possible save you when this all takes place? I will tell you, nothing except a sincere relationship with our Lord and Saviour Jesus Christ.

Is Jesus coming alone?

> *"And He shall send His angels with a great sound of a trumpet, and they shall gather together His elect from the four winds, from one end of heaven to the other." Matthew 24:31*

> *"When the Son of man shall come in His glory, and all the holy angels with Him, then shall He sit upon the throne of His glory." Matthew 25:31*

"...and the number of them was ten thousand times ten thousand, and thousands of thousands." Revelation 5:11

Reader, this is amazing for all the holy angels will be coming with Him. Remember what God's Word has to say:

"And, behold, there was a great earthquake: for the angel of the Lord descended from heaven, and came and rolled back the stone from the door, and sat upon it. His countenance was like lightning, and his raiment white as snow." Matthew 28:2, 3

The earth quaked from one angel and his appearance was as lightning can you imagine how it will be with all the holy angels coming with Jesus.

This event will be visual, loud, and very overwhelming with all that will be taking place. Don't be fooled!

Will Jesus Christ touch the earth when He comes the second time?

No, the Word of God says:

"For the Lord Himself shall descend from heaven with a shout, with the voice of the archangel, and with the trump of God: and the dead in Christ shall rise first: Then we which are alive [and] remain shall be caught up together with them in the clouds, to meet the Lord in the air: and so shall we ever be with the Lord. Wherefore comfort one another with these words." I Thessalonians 4:16–18

The Bible is clear, the angels will gather God's people (*Matthew 24:31*), and they will be caught up into the air to meet Jesus there.

Many people have asked the question in regards to our bodies, when we go to heaven will we be some spirit or what? Let's look at the Bible for this answer as well.

> *"And as they thus spake, Jesus Himself stood in the midst of them, and saith unto them, Peace [be] unto you. But they were terrified and affrighted, and supposed that they had seen a spirit. And He said unto them, Why are ye troubled? and why do thoughts arise in your hearts? Behold My hands and My feet, that it is I Myself: handle Me, and see; for a spirit hath not flesh and bones, as ye see Me have. And when He had thus spoken, He showed them [His] hands and [His] feet. And while they yet believed not for joy, and wondered, He said unto them, Have ye here any meat? And they gave Him a piece of a broiled fish, and of an honeycomb. And He took [it], and did eat before them." Luke 24:36–43*

That is exciting! Jesus wanted to make it clear that after the resurrection, a person will have flesh and bones, and yes, we will still be able to eat food.

> *"Now this I say, brethren, that flesh and blood cannot inherit the kingdom of God; neither doth corruption inherit incorruption. Behold, I show you a mystery; We shall not all sleep, but we shall all be changed, In a moment, in the twinkling of an eye, at the last trump: for the trumpet shall sound, and the dead shall be raised incorruptible, and we shall be changed. For this*

corruptible must put on incorruption, and this mortal [must] put on immortality." I Corinthians 15:50–53

It is Jesus Christ who:

"Shall change our vile body, that it may be fashioned like unto His glorious body, according to the working whereby He is able even to subdue all things unto Himself." Philippians 3:21

What good news; the glorious coming of Jesus Christ is soon to take place. So my friends:

"Work out your own salvation with fear and trembling. For it is God which worketh in you both to will and to do of [His] good pleasure. Do all things without murmurings and disputings: That ye may be blameless and harmless, the sons of God, without rebuke, in the midst of a crooked and perverse nation, among whom ye shine as lights in the world." Philippians 2:12–15

—Twenty-six—
What Happens When You Die?

This is a very interesting question considering that when Jesus comes He will be resurrecting the righteous dead to take back to heaven with Him. So many people today have been misinformed regarding this topic. This is truly one of the biggest deceptions that Satan has laid before mankind. Let's go to our only guide that will not deceive us and is very plain in regards to this topic.

Let's start with how man was created.

"And the LORD God formed man [of] the dust of the ground, and breathed into his nostrils the breath of life; and man became a living soul." Genesis 2:7

Please note that it was after the breath of God entered into the man that he became a living soul. The soul did not exist until the man was formed from the dust and then God put His breath into the man, and then man became a living soul.

What is a "soul?"

We can see that from *Genesis 2:7,* the soul is a living being. A soul is always a combination of two things; body, plus breath. A soul cannot exist unless these two elements are combined together. God's Word teaches that we are a living soul.

"Then they that gladly received his word were baptized: and the same day there were added [unto them] about three thousand souls." Acts 2:41

"If a soul sin, and commit a trespass against the LORD *..." Leviticus 6:2*

Again the Bible is referring to the living being as the soul.

"Let him know, that he which converteth the sinner from the error of his way shall save a soul from death, and shall hide a multitude of sins." James 5:20

Do souls die?

"The soul that sinneth, it shall die." Ezekiel 18:20

"... and every living soul died in the sea." Revelation 16:3

God's Word tells us that souls do die, and we are souls. Man is mortal according to *Job 4:17;* the word "immortal" is only used in the Bible one time and it refers to God.

"Now unto the King eternal, immortal, invisible, the only wise God, [be] honour and glory for ever and ever. Amen." I Timothy 1:17

Reader, I also encourage you to look up the word "soul" in the Bible and you will see that it refers to the body, persons, or creatures. Not some ghostly spirit that goes off someplace after a person dies. The teaching that the soul is undying and immortal goes against the Bible. The Bible teaches that the soul is subject to death.

Do good people go to heaven when they die?

The Bible teaches that you go to your grave.

"... all that are in the graves shall hear His voice ... And shall come forth ..." John 5:28, 29

"Men [and] brethren, let me freely speak unto you of the patriarch David, that he is both dead and buried, and his sepulchre is with us unto this day ... For David is not ascended into the heavens." Acts 2:29, 34

"If I wait, the grave [is] mine house." Job 17:13

So what happens to a person when they die?

"Then shall the dust return to the earth as it was: and the spirit shall return unto God who gave it." Ecclesiastes 12:7

The word spirit here in Hebrew means breath. (See *the Strong's Concordance of the Bible, #7307)* So once a person dies, the body returns to the dust and the spirit, (breath) returns to God who gave it.

"If He set his heart upon man, [if] He gather unto himself his spirit and his breath; All flesh shall perish together, and man shall turn again unto dust." Job 34:14, 15

Now the Bible has made it clear that the combination of both the dust and the breath of God make man a living soul. So it makes perfectly good sense that one these two elements return to their origin, the soul would no longer exist. After death everything seems to go back from whence it came. Death is just the opposite of creation. The psalmist describes death in these words:

"Thou takest away their breath; they die, and return to their dust. Thou sendest forth Thy spirit, they are created." Psalms 104:29, 30

So is it possible for a person that is dead to comprehend anything after death?

"For the living know that they shall die: but the dead know not any thing, neither have they any more a reward; for the memory of them is forgotten. Also their love, and their hatred, and their envy, is now perished; neither have they any more a portion for ever in any [thing] that is done under the sun." Ecclesiastes 9:5, 6

"The dead praise not the LORD." Psalms 115:17

The dead cannot contact the living, nor do they know what the living are doing. They are dead.

"So man lieth down, and riseth not: till the heavens [be] no more, they shall not awake, nor be raised out of their sleep … His sons come to honour, and he knoweth [it] not; and they are brought low, but he perceiveth [it] not of them." Job 14:12, 21

"His breath goeth forth, he returneth to his earth; in that very day his thoughts perish." Psalms 146:4

"For the grave cannot praise Thee, death can [not] celebrate thee: they that go down into the pit cannot hope for Thy truth." Isaiah 38:18

"For in death [there is] no remembrance of Thee: in the grave who shall give Thee thanks?" Psalms 6:5

"So man lieth down, and riseth not: till the heavens [be] no more, they shall not awake, nor be raised out of their sleep." Job 14:12

Reader, as you can see, the heavens are still here, and you can see also that the Bible relates death to sleep. You can find in the Old Testament the phrase "*slept with his fathers*" many times, referring to someone that had died and was buried.

In the New Testament Jesus Himself refers to death as sleep. Let's review this.

Lazarus had died. Jesus said to His disciples:

"Our friend Lazarus sleepeth; but I go, that I may awake him out of sleep. Then said his disciples, Lord, if he sleep, he shall do well. Howbeit Jesus spake of his death: but they thought that he had spoken of taking of rest in sleep. Then said Jesus unto them plainly, Lazarus is dead." John 11:11–14

Here is a classic example of the true Bible teaching about death. Christ called death a sleep. Later, He stood by the rock-hewn sepulchre of His friend and cried out, "*Lazarus, come forth*!" (*John 11:43*) He did not say, "Lazarus, come down." Lazarus was not up in heaven, nor was he anywhere else, except inside the walls of his tomb. In response to the call of Jesus, he awoke from his sleep of death and:

"... came forth, bound hand and foot with graveclothes: and his face was bound about with a napkin. Jesus saith unto them, Loose him, and let him go." John 11:44

So let's take a look at what happens to the righteous dead at the second coming of Jesus Christ.

"Behold, I come quickly; and my reward [is] with me, to give every man according as his work shall be." Revelation 22:12

"For the Lord Himself shall descend from heaven with a shout, with the voice of the archangel, and with the trump of God: and the dead in Christ shall rise first: Then we which are alive [and] remain shall be caught up together with them in the clouds, to meet the Lord in the air: and so shall we ever be with the Lord." I Thessalonians 4:16, 17

"Behold, I show you a mystery; We shall not all sleep, but we shall all be changed, In a moment, in the twinkling of an eye, at the last trump: for the trumpet shall sound, and the dead shall be raised incorruptible, and we shall be changed. For this corruptible must put on incorruption, and this mortal [must] put on immortality." I Corinthians 15:51–53

So they shall be rewarded. They will be raised, and given immortal bodies, and caught up to meet the Lord in the air. Please think about this for a moment. If you died and went directly to heaven or hell what need would there be for a resurrection? Jesus said that He would raise us up at the last day. (See *John 6:39, 40, 44, 54*) This will be at His second coming.

What was the Devil's first lie?

"And the serpent said unto the woman, Ye shall not surely die." Genesis 3:4

"That old serpent, called the Devil, and Satan." Revelation 12:9

Satan told Eve that sin would not bring death. *"Ye shall not surely die,"* he said. This is one of the devil's biggest deceptions that he holds over mankind. The Bible gives us examples of how he (Satan) has worked powerful miracles down through the ages through people who claim to receive their power from the spirits of the dead. Satan will use all types of witchcraft to deceive people. (See *Exodus 7:11*—magicians of Egypt; *1 Samuel 28:3–25*—woman of Endor; *Daniel* 2:2—sorcerers; *Acts 16:16–18*—a certain damsel.)

Can Satan and the fallen angels work miracles?

The Bible says:

"For they are the spirits of devils, working miracles." Revelation 16:14

"For there shall arise false Christs, and false prophets, and shall show great signs and wonders; insomuch that, if [it were] possible, they shall deceive the very elect." Matthew 24:24

Yes, the Bible is very clear. The Devil will work very convincing miracles. (See *Revelation 13:13, 14* and *2 Corinthians 11:13–15.*)

"And no marvel; for Satan himself is transformed into an angel of light." II Corinthians 11:14

But we have been warned before hand. (See *Matthew 24:23, 24.*) Keep in mind that these deceptions will be so convincing and seem so spiritual that those who believe the dead are alive, in any form, will most assuredly be deceived. The universal feeling will be that Christ and His angels are leading out in a fantastic worldwide revival. The entire emphasis will seem so spiritual and be so supernatural that only God's elect will not be deceived.

So why will God's people not be deceived?

"They received the Word with all readiness of mind, and searched the Scriptures daily, whether those things were so." Acts 17:11

"To the Law and to the testimony: if they speak not according to this Word, [it is] because [there is] no light in them." Isaiah 8:20

God's children will search the Scriptures diligently allowing the true Holy Spirit to lead them.

How does God regard those that teach that the dead are alive? Is He serious about this topic?

"A man also or woman that hath a familiar spirit, or that is a wizard, shall surely be put to death." Leviticus 20:27

Also see *Galatians 5:19–21* on witchcraft. The *Webster's Dictionary* tells us that witchcraft is practice of magic and a wizard is a magician.

"But the fearful, and unbelieving, and the abominable, and murderers, and whoremongers, and sorcerers, and idolaters, and all liars, shall have their part in the lake which burneth with fire and brimstone." Revelation 21:8

God is very serious about this. All those who practice, involve themselves, and teach others these things will be destroyed.

For more on this topic and many others send off for you free *Amazing Facts* Studies today.

—Twenty-seven—

The Biblical Sabbath—Saturday or Sunday?

I often wonder if the Christian people of today know why they worship on Sunday. As the Lord led me in the study of the prophecies of *Daniel* and *Revelation*, I found out some very interesting statements made by church leaders throughout history in regards to which day is the true Sabbath. I would like to list some of them, but there are more than what you will read here. Reader, please keep in mind that this is not my opinion and I am not making this up. All quotes will list their source.

Baptist

"There was and is a commandment to keep holy the Sabbath day but that Sabbath day was not Sunday ... It will be said, however, and with some show of triumph, that the Sabbath was transferred from the seventh to the first day of the week ... Where can the record of such a transaction be found? Not in the New Testament - absolutely not. There is no scriptural evidence of the change of the Sabbath institution from the seventh to the first day of the week." From a paper by Dr. Edward T. Hiscox, author of The Baptist Manual.

Methodist

"Take the matter of Sunday ... there is no passage telling Christians to keep that day, or to transfer the Jewish Sabbath to that day." - Harris Franklin Fall, Christian Advocate, July 2, 1942.

Presbyterian

"The Christian Sabbath (Sunday) is not in the Scriptures, and was not by the primitive Church called the Sabbath." Dwight's Theology, vol. 4, pg. 401

Episcopal

"Is there any command is the New Testament to change the day of weekly rest from Saturday to Sunday? None." Manual of Christian Doctrine, pg. 127

Church of Christ

"I do believe that the Lord's Day came in the place of the Jewish Sabbath, or the first day for the seventh, is absolutely without any authority in the New Testament." Alexander Campbell, Washington Reporter, October 8, 1821

Congregationalist

"The current notion that Christ and His apostles authoritatively substituted the first day for the seventh, is absolutely without any authority in the New Testament." Dr. Lyman Abbott, Christian Union, January 19, 1882

Christian

"There never was any change of the Sabbath from Saturday to Sunday. There is not in any place in the Bible any intimation of such a change." First-Day Observance, pg. 17, 19

Lutheran

"The observance of the Lord's day (Sunday) is founded not on any command of God, but on the <u>authority of the</u>

church." Augsburg Confession of Faith, quoted in Catholic Sabbath Manual, part 2, chapter 1, section 10.

Reader, did you catch that last statement?—"On the authority of the church." There is no church that has authority over God that has the power to change the Commandments of God. Is man to instruct God? I think not, but there is a church that exalts herself to believe she does, and just about the whole Christian world pays homage to that church by accepting her day of worship in place of the Biblical day of worship given by the Commandment of God. Let's take a look at what this church has to say in regards to this.

Roman Catholic Church

"You may read the Bible from Genesis to Revelation, and you will not find a single line authorizing the sanctification of Sunday. The Scriptures enforce the religious observance of Saturday, a day which we (Catholics) never sanctify." James Cardinal Gibbons, The Faith of Our Fathers, pg. 111

"It is well to remind the Presbyterians, Baptists, Methodists, and all other Christians, that the Bible does not support them anywhere in their observance of Sunday. Sunday is an institution of the Roman Catholic Church and those who observe the day observe a commandment of the Catholic Church." Priest Brady, in an address at Elizabeth, N. J., March 17, 1903; reported in the Elizabeth, N. J., News of March 18, 1903.

"If Protestants would follow the Bible, they should worship God on the Sabbath day. In keeping the Sunday they are following a law of the Catholic Church." Albert Smith, Chancellor of the Archdiocese of Baltimore, replying for the Cardinal, in a letter of February 10, 1920.

"Prove to me from the Bible alone that I am bound to keep Sunday holy. There is no law in the Bible. It is a law of the holy Catholic Church alone. The Bible says, "Remember the Sabbath day to keep it holy." The Catholic Church says, No—by my divine power I abolish the Sabbath day and command you to keep holy the first day of the week. And lo! The entire civilized world bows down in reverent obedience to the command of the holy Catholic Church." Priest Thomas Enright, CSSR, President of Redemptorist College, Kansas City, Mo. in a lecture at Hartford, Kansas Weekly Call, February 22, 1884, and the American Sentinel, a New York Roman Catholic journal, in June 1893, pg. 173

"Of course the Catholic Church claims that the change was her act ... AND THE ACT IS A ***MARK*** *of her ecclesiastical power." From the office of Cardinal Gibbons, through Chancellor H.F. Thomas, November 11, 1895.*

And why does this Church claim this so boldly?

"We hold upon this earth the place of God Almighty." Pope Leo X111, Encyclical Letter, June 20, 1894. The Great Encyclical Letters of Leo XIII, pg. 304.

Reader, as you can see, not one of these churches claim that God changed the Sabbath Day. As you have observed, the change is claimed to be made by the Roman Catholic Church which claims to stand in the place of God. I don't know about you, reader, but I believe in Jesus Christ to be the way, the truth, and the life. (*John 14.6*) There is neither man nor church on this earth that has the authority to change the Law of God. If the Commandments of God could have been changed Jesus Christ would not have had to come down from heaven and die on the cross for our sins in order to redeem us.

Roman Catholic authorities claim the Seventh Day Adventist Church is the only major Protestant denomination keeping Holy the true Sabbath as taught in the Bible.

> *"The [Catholic) Church changed the observance of the Sabbath to Sunday by right of the divine, infallible authority given to her by her Founder, Jesus Christ. The Protestant, claiming the Bible to be the only guide of faith, has no warrant for observing Sunday. In this matter the Seventh Day Adventist is the only consistent Protestant." The Question Box, The Catholic Universe Bulletin, August 14, 1942, pg. 4*

> *"The Israelite respects the authority of the Old Testament only, but the [Seventh-Day] Adventist, who is a Christian, accepts the New Testament on the same ground as the old, viz.: and inspired record also. He finds that the Bible, His teacher, is consistent in both parts; that the Redeemer, during His mortal life, never kept any other day than Saturday. The Gospels plainly evince to him this fact; whilst, in the pages of the Acts of the Apostles, the Epistles and the Apocalypse, not the vestige of an act canceling the Saturday arrangement can be found." Editorial, The Catholic Mirror (Baltimore), September 2, 1893*

> *"You may read the Bible from Genesis to Revelation, and you will not find a single line authorizing the sanctification of Sunday. The Scriptures enforce the religious observance of Saturday, a day which we never sanctioned." Cardinal Gibbons (for many years head of the Catholic Church in America), The Faith of Our Fathers 92"d erg, rev. pg. 89*

"Nowhere in the Bible do we find that Christ or the Apostles ordered that the Sabbath be changed from Saturday to Sunday. We have the commandment of God given to Moses to keep Holy the Sabbath Day, that is the 7th day of the week, Saturday. Today most Christians keep Sunday because it has been revealed to us by the [Catholic] Church outside the Bible." —To Tell You the Truth, The Catholic Virginian, October 3, 1947, pg. 9

You may be thinking that the Bible Sabbath is for the Jews only, for I have heard pastors as well as other people say this. So let's take a look at the Bible to see if it was for the Jews only. This is the safest and most reliable source to let the Bible interpret itself.

1) "*God blessed the seventh day and sanctified it.*" (*Genesis 2:3*), this was before sin happened. Note Sanctified means, "to set apart for holy use." The only ones in the Garden of Eden to "sanctify" the Sabbath were Adam and Eve, who were not Jewish.
2) Jesus said, "*the Sabbath was made for man.*" The Sabbath day of rest was established in the Garden of Eden before it was written on Mount Sinai. Jesus makes it all clear when He says, "*the Sabbath was made for man*" (*Mark 2:27*), not just for the Jews.
3) God wrote the "Ten Commandments" on stone, not just nine. See *Deuteronomy 10:1–5*. Adultery, murder, stealing, lying and idol worship Commandments were not given just for the Jews. So then why should the Fourth Commandment just be for the Jews?
4) "*The seventh day is the Sabbath of the Lord thy God.*" (*Exodus 20:10*). God calls it, "*My Holy Day*" (*Isaiah 58:13*). The Bible never calls it "The Sabbath

for the Jews." It is not their Sabbath. It is God's and He made it for man.

5) The Sabbath Commandment is for the stranger too. The Fourth Commandment itself says the "stranger" is to rest on the Sabbath (*Exodus 20:10*). Strangers are Gentiles, read *Isaiah 56:6.*

6) Isaiah said Gentiles should keep the Sabbath. It states, "*also the sons of the stranger ... every one that keepth the Sabbath ... for Mine house shall be called an house of prayer for all people*" (*Isaiah 56:6, 7*).

7) "*All*" mankind will keep the Sabbath in the New Earth. "*From one Sabbath to another, shall all flesh come to worship before Me, saith the Lord*" (*Isaiah 66:22, 23*). Here again the Bible makes it clear "*all flesh,*" not just Jews. So reader, why not start now?

8) Gentiles kept the Sabbath in the Book of Acts. "*The Gentiles besought that these words might be preached to them the next Sabbath.*" Please note: if Sunday was for the Gentiles, they would have besought that these words be preached the next day (Sunday) not the next Sabbath. Paul and Barnabas ... persuaded them to continue in the grace of God. See *Acts 13:42, 43.*

10) "*The whole law*" is for "*all the world*" not just for the Jews. James and Paul wrote these words. Read *Romans 3:19; James 2:10, 11.*

All these passages make it clear that the Sabbath is not just for the Jews as some pastors and people say. It is for all mankind. So far we have come to understand that the Biblical Sabbath is Saturday and not Sunday, and that the Sabbath which is the seventh day, not the first day, was made by God for all people, not just for the Jews.

Now let's look at some of the common reasons against the Sabbath. Are they really right or are they taken out of context.

Some quote the following words to prove that the Sabbath was only for Israel, "*Speak thou also unto the children of Israel, saying, Verily My Sabbaths ye shall keep: for it is a sign between Me and you ... it is a sign between Me and the children of Israel forever: for in six days the Lord made heaven and the earth, and on the seventh day He rested*" (*Exodus 31:13, 17*).

Notice that God said "*My Sabbaths*" will endure "*forever.*" The reason goes back to Creation, before Israel existed. Isaiah said the Gentiles who joined the Jews were also to keep the Sabbath (*Isaiah 56:6*). Paul wrote to the Gentiles, "*If ye be Christ's then are ye Abraham's seed.*" (*Galatians 3:29*) Gentiles are "*grafted in*" (*Romans 11:17*). Therefore, the sign is for them too. Gentiles in the book of Acts kept the Sabbath. (*Acts 13:42–44*) The saving covenant is never made with anyone but Israel. (See *Hebrews 8:10.*)

Is the Creation Sabbath the same as "the Sabbaths which are a shadow of things to come," in Colossians 2:14–17?

This is one of the most misused passages in the entire New Testament. "*Blotting out the handwriting of ordinances that was against us ... nailing it to His cross*" (*verse 14*). The law that was "*blotted out*" and nailed to the cross was not the Ten Commandments. See *Luke 16:17, 18; Romans 7:7, 12; James 2:10–12*. It was the "*handwriting*" of the "*law*" of sacrifices written by "*Moses*" in "*a book*" which was a continual witness against Israel (*Deuteronomy 31:24–26*).

This law of sacrifices was "*against them,*" because its very existence was a witness that they had broken the Ten Commandments. That's why then needed to offer lambs.

"Therefore," wrote Paul in *Colossians 2:16*, *"let no man therefore judge you in meat, or in drink, or in respect of an holy day, or of the new moon, or of the Sabbath days which are a shadow of things to come"* (*Verses 16, 17*). Paul here refers to the Jewish *"feasts ... meat offerings ... drink offerings,"* AND YEARLY "*SABBATHS*" OF THE CEREMONIAL LAW. Leviticus 23:37, 24, 32, 38.

These yearly Sabbaths, like the Passover and the Day of Atonement, were "*shadows*" pointing forward to Jesus Christ. *Hebrews 10:1* also affirms that it was the ceremonial law with its yearly Sabbaths and "*sacrifices*" that were a shadow.

Therefore, the Ten Commandments and the creation Sabbath are NOT A SHADOW pointing forward to Jesus. The seventh day Sabbath POINTS BACK to the creation of the world and remains in the New Testament. (See *Matthew 24:20; Luke 23:56.*) Paul also continued to keep the Sabbath, *Acts 16:13.*

Now let's look at Romans 14:5: "One man esteemeth one day above another; another esteemeth every day alike."

To begin with, it must be admitted that the word "Sabbath" is not found in the entire chapter. People assume Paul is talking about the Sabbath. But is he really? The chapter begins with, "*Him that is weak in the faith receive ye, but not to doubtful disputations*" (*verse 1*). The *NKJV* reads, "*disputes over doubtful things.*" Note this chapter concerns "*doubtful things*" and is not a discussion of the Ten Commandments. The Ten Commandments are not "*doubtful*" but exceedingly clear, for they were written with the finger of God on two tables of stone (*Exodus 31:18*).

The "*weak*" brother "*eats*" some things and "*esteems one day above another,*" while the strong brother believes that he may "*eat all things*" and "*esteems every day alike*"

(*Romans 14:2, 5*). The early Church was made up of Jewish believers and Gentile converts. Although Paul did not specify what "days" he was referring to, he was probably talking about the "*esteeming*" or "*not esteeming*" of certain Jewish fast or feast days. (See *Luke 18:12*, and *Leviticus 23:2.*) There were also certain pagan feast days when people were especially eating of those things that were offered in sacrifice unto idols (*1 Corinthians 8:4*).

A "strong" Jew who knew that "*an idol is nothing*," would have no scruples about eating "meat in an idol temple" on a pagan feast day. (*I Corinthians 8:4, 10.*) Paul warned these "strong" Jewish believers:

> *"But take heed lest by any means this liberty of yours become a stumblingblock to them that are weak. For if any man see thee which hast knowledge sit at meat in the idol's temple, shall not the conscience of him which is weak be emboldened to eat those things which are offered to idols; And through thy knowledge shall the weak brother perish, for whom Christ died? But when ye sin so against the brethren, and wound their weak conscience, ye sin against Christ. Wherefore, if meat make my brother to offend, I will eat no flesh while the world standeth …" I Corinthians 8:9–13*

THERE IS NO EVIDENCE that the discussion about "*the weak and the strong*" in *Romans chapter 14*, and *I Corinthians chapter 8*, has ANYTHING TO DO WITH THE SABBATH. God has never said, "One man may choose to esteem My Sabbath, while another man may choose to esteem Sunday, or every day alike." He has not left it up to us to "pick a day, any day." Rather, God has commanded:

"Remember the Sabbath day to keep it holy … the seventh day is the Sabbath of the Lord thy God." Exodus 20:8, 10

The book of Romans is very clear:

"By the Law is the knowledge of sin." Romans 3:20

Let's take a look at another passage that is often quoted: "You observe days, and months, and times, and years. I am afraid of you." Galatians 4:10, 11

Would Christians ever apply these words to Sunday? The context refers to the past pagan lives of these converts.

"Then, when ye knew not God, ye did service unto them which by nature are no gods. But now … how turn ye again to the weak and beggarly elements, whereunto ye desire again to be in bondage? Ye observe days, and months, and times, and years." Galatians 4:8–10

The Galatians were turning "*again*" to idolatry. They must have been slipping back into the observance of pagan "*days, months, times, and years*." They were also under attack from certain Jewish believers who wanted them to be circumcised and keep the Law of Moses. (*Galatians 2:3, 4; Acts 15:1.*)

These Jewish believers were probably commanding them to keep the Jewish feasts of the ceremonial law (Passover, etc.) which Paul clearly speaks on in *Colossians 2:14–17*. The "*weak and beggarly elements*" leading to "*bondage*" were not the Ten Commandments. The Ten Commandment Law is "*the royal law … the law of liberty*" (*James 2:8–12*).

So is the Sabbath Day important to God?

Yes it is, read *Ezekiel 22:26; Jeremiah 17:19–27; Isaiah 58:13*. You probably have also heard that you should worship every day, and yes, we should spend time communing with God everyday; but only the seventh day is the Sabbath of the Lord (*Exodus 20:10*). You may be thinking, "But Jesus Christ rose on Sunday." Praise the Lord! But let's not use the resurrection as a reason for breaking one of the Ten Commandments (THE SABBATH). Jesus never mentioned Sunday. Baptism is the ceremony to honor the resurrection.

> *"Therefore we are buried with Him by baptism into death: that like as Christ was raised up from the dead by the glory of the Father, even so we also should walk in newness of life." Romans 6:4*

I am sure the you have heard pastors and people say that we are not under the law but under grace.

True, but don't forget to read the next verse which says:

> *"What then? shall we sin, because we are not under the law, but under grace? God forbid." Romans 6:15*

> *"Sin is the transgression of the law." I John 3:4*

Jesus saves us from sin (*Matthew 1:21*). You see, reader, so many people do not continue to search to understand in full what the Word of God is saying. So much these days is being taken out of context.

Now you're probably thinking, "Can so many people be wrong?" Why did only 8 people enter the ark? "Majority opinion," is not our guide.

The Bible tells us:

"Thou shalt not follow a multitude to [do] evil." Exodus 23:2

Listen to what Jesus has to say:

"Enter ye in at the strait gate: for wide [is] the gate, and broad [is] the way, that leadeth to destruction, and many there be which go in thereat: Because strait [is] the gate, and narrow [is] the way, which leadeth unto life, and few there be that find it." Matthew 7:13, 14

Jesus also told a group of "very religious people," that they were "*making the Word of God of none effect*" through ***"TRADITION"*** *(Mark 7:13).*

Many "good people" have never studied this subject carefully. So let's examine each of the 8 Scriptures in the New Testament that mention Sunday, "the first day of the week."

1. *Matthew 28:1—"In the end of the Sabbath, as it began to dawn toward the first day of the week."* Note here two different days are mentioned, one is "*the Sabbath*," and the other is "*the first day of the week*," or Sunday. Jesus Christ rose from the dead on Sunday, but *Matthew* reveals that this did not make Sunday the Sabbath.
2. *Mark 6:1, 2—"When the Sabbath was past ... very early in the morning the first day of the week."* The resurrection of Jesus on Sunday morning was glorious. Super-glorious! Yet, there is no evidence that this made Sunday sacred. Did the cross make Friday

sacred? As in *Matthew 28:1*, Sunday came "*when the Sabbath was past*," that is, the day after Sabbath.

3. *Mark 16:9—"Jesus was risen early the first day of the week.*" Sunday is simply called "*the first day of the week.*" The "*week*" began in Genesis at Creation. God made the world in six literal days, and He "*rested on the seventh day … blessed the seventh day, and sanctified it*" (*Genesis 2:2, 3*). God made "the seventh day" HIS HOLY DAY, not "*the first day of the week.*"
4. *Luke 24:1—"The women went to the tomb on the first day of the week," after "they rested the Sabbath day, according to the commandment*" (*Luke 23:56*). This text is extremely important. These were Christian women. They loved Jesus. They kept the Sabbath after the cross. Luke was a Gentile who wrote this about 28 years after the resurrection. The Sabbath was still there. These women were keeping it "*according to the commandment*" found in *Exodus 20:8–11.* These verses prove that the Sabbath continued after the cross, and that the Sabbath is not Sunday.
5. *John 20:1—"Mary came to the tomb on the first day of the week.*" As in *Matthew*, *Mark*, and *Luke*, *John* simply gives a narrative account of the resurrection of our Lord on Sunday the first day of the week.
6. *John 20:19—"On the first day of the week*" (late Sunday afternoon), the disciples "*were assembled*" behind shut doors. Why? "*For fear of the Jews.*" This was not a worship service. They were afraid. They had not believed the reports from the women that Jesus had risen. (See *Mark 16:9–13.*) Did they think that the Jewish authorities might burst in, accuse them of stealing the body, and then arrest them? Then Jesus revealed Himself as the risen Lord; yet, he never mentioned Sunday.

7. *I Corinthians 16:2—"Concerning the collection for the saints"* (*vs. 1*). This text and other Scriptural references, reveals that Paul was raising a "*collection*" (not a tithe), for the needy believers in "*Jerusalem*" (*vs. 3*) during a time of famine. (See *Acts 11:27–30; Romans 15:25, 26.*) On "*the first day of the week*" (Sunday), "*let every one*" (individually), "*lay by him*" (Lit. Greek "at home"), "*in store*" a certain amount. The Greek "*by him in store*" reveals that this was to be done in their homes. The first day of the week was ideal for the Corinthian believers to look back on the previous week, examine their finances, and set aside a weekly contribution. This would then be gathered and made ready for Paul, "*that there be no gathering when I come.*" Paul was going to pass through Corinth. He wanted the money ready for him to pick up. The request to dispense with "gathering," indicates this first day of the week "was not a day of worship."
8. *Acts 20:6–13*—This was Paul's last meeting with a small group of believers in "*Troas.*" It was night (*20:7, 8*), on the "*first day of the week.*" Biblically, the day begins at sunset. (*Genesis 1:5, 8; Luke 23:54.*) Therefore, this meeting took place on a Saturday night. The *New English Bible* says, "*On Saturday night.*" They "*broke bread,*" which the early believers did "*daily*" (*Acts 2:46*). Paul preached his farewell sermon, "*ready to depart on the morrow.*" Sunday morning, at the "*break of day,*" while Luke "*sailed,*" Paul began his 25-mile trip to Troas for "*seven days*" (*vs. 6*). A simple count reveals that they arrived on the previous Sunday, stayed for a week, and had their last meeting on that Saturday night, which would have been a continuation after the Sabbath. Not far from Troas, Paul kept the Sabbath (*Acts 16:11–13*). The book of

Acts mentions Sunday only one time, yet, the Sabbath is mentioned eleven times (*1:12; 13:14, 27, 42, 44; 15:21; 16:13; 17:2; 18:4*). A careful study of this "Saturday Night in Troas—Sunday Travel to Assos," account is proof that Paul did not keep Sunday holy, for he traveled a great distance on that day.

Now let's look at seven facts:

1. Sunday is simply called, "*the first day of the week.*"
2. Jesus Christ Himself never mentioned Sunday, not even one time!
3. Not once is Sunday set aside as a Holy Day in honor of the resurrection.
4. In *Matthew, Mark*, and *Luke*, Sunday always comes "*after the Sabbath.*"
5. The Holy Spirit comes to teach only what Jesus taught, *John 14:26; 16:13, 14.* Because Jesus never mentioned Sunday, the Holy Spirit will not teach it.
6. The apostles were to teach only what Jesus "*commanded*" (*Matthew 28:20*). Because Jesus never mentioned Sunday, the apostles could not have taught it.
7. Sunday cannot be a part of the New Covenant, because it began after the blood was shed (*Matthew 26:28*). After death, you cannot add to a covenant. (See *Galatians 3:15; Hebrews 9:16, 17*).

The Sabbath was made by Christ, for He made all things:

"Without Him was not any thing made that was made."
John 1:3

It was made for man:

> *"The Sabbath was made for man." Mark 2:27*

Reader, it is clear that the observance of Sunday is the tradition of men. Jesus said:

> *"In vain do they worship Me, teaching [for] doctrines the commandments of men. For laying aside the Commandment of God, ye hold the tradition of men." Mark 7:7, 8*

Satan has set up a counterfeit for everything that God has done to draw people away from the true worship of God to himself, and so here we see a counterfeit Sabbath. The origin of Sunday observance was introduced by the Roman Catholic Church, we see that they openly admitted this. Any Protestant church that accepts the belief that Sunday is to be kept in place of the 7th day Sabbath of the Bible (Old and New Testament) is showing allegiance to the Papacy (Roman Catholic Church).

It saddens my heart to see so many sincere Christians blinded by the traditions of men that they would grieve the Holy Spirit when shown what Jesus Christ would have them to do. May not one think in his heart that God will deal lightly with those that have been shown the truth from the Bible; and yet, openly choose to follow Satan's counterfeit day of worship. The mark of our allegiance to God as having creative authority is in the observance of the Sabbath, from sundown Friday to sundown Saturday. The mark of one's allegiance to the traditions of men would be to accept Sunday, or any other day of worship in place of the 4th Commandment given by God.

"Remember the Sabbath day, to keep it holy. Six days shalt thou labour, and do all thy work: But the seventh day [is] the Sabbath of the Lord thy God: [in it] thou shalt not do any work, thou, nor thy son, nor thy daughter, thy manservant, nor thy maidservant, nor thy cattle, nor thy stranger that [is] within thy gates: For [in] six days the Lord made heaven and earth, the sea, and all that in them [is], and rested the seventh day: wherefore the Lord blessed the Sabbath day, and hallowed it." Exodus 20:8–11

When did God begin our days?

"And the evening and the morning were the first day." Genesis 1:5

The day God designated in which His true followers should acknowledge and worship Him as the Creator, is the evening and morning of the 7th day Sabbath.

Reader, pray with me: "Eternal Father, we thank Thee for Thy Word, we thank Thee for revealing to us how the enemy has set up a counterfeit day of worship. We ask Thee to give us the grace that we may keep Thy true Sabbath according to Thy 4th Commandment; that we may honor Thee. We thank Thee for Thy Son Jesus Christ, that paid the price on Calvary by dying on the cross the death we deserve. We thank Thee, Father, for winking at our ignorance and suffering long with us in regards to this matter and many others. And now that the truth has been revealed, we ask Thee to help us apply the Word to our lives that we many walk in harmony with Thee. We are thankful for the quietness of this place, we can hear You calling to our hearts, *"Come unto Me, all [ye] that labour and are heavy laden, and I will give you rest." (Matthew 11:28)* We thank Thee that there is a rest that remains to the people of God. Give us the grace and power to enter into this Sabbath rest. We ask through Jesus Christ our Lord. Amen"

Jesus says:

"My sheep hear My voice, and I know them, and they follow Me." John 10:27

"But the hour cometh, and now is, when the true worshippers shall worship the Father in spirit and in truth: for the Father seeketh such to worship him. God [is] a Spirit: and they that worship Him ***must*** *worship [Him] in* ***spirit and in truth****." John 4:23, 24*

So I encourage you to choose you this day whom ye will serve.

"Know ye not, that to whom ye yield yourselves servants to obey, his servants ye are to whom ye obey; whether of sin unto death, or of obedience unto righteousness?" Romans 6:16

Jesus said:

"If ye love Me, keep My commandments ... He that hath My commandments, and keepeth them, he it is that loveth Me: and he that loveth Me shall be loved of My Father, and I will love him, and will manifest Myself to him." John 14:15, 21

Let our prayer be to Jesus:

"Create in me a clean heart, O God; and renew a right spirit within me ... Teach me, O LORD, the way of Thy statutes; and I shall keep it [unto] the end. Give me

understanding, and I shall keep Thy Law; yea, I shall observe it with [my] whole heart. Make me to go in the path of Thy Commandments; for therein do I delight … Let Thy mercies come also unto me, O Lord, [even] Thy salvation, according to Thy Word." Psalms 51:10; 119:33–35, 41

Reader, when Jesus speaks of the new heart, He means the mind, the life, the whole being. To have a change of heart is to withdraw the affections from the world, and fasten them upon Christ. To have a clean heart is to have a new mind, new purposes, and new motives. What is a sign of a new heart?—a changed life. There is a daily, hourly dying to selfishness and pride. We are to receive the new heart that is kept soft and tender by the grace of heaven. The selfish spirit is to be cleanses from the soul. We are to labor earnestly and with humility of heart, each one looking to Jesus for guidance and encouragement.

"Happy [is] the man [that] findeth wisdom, and the man [that] getteth understanding." Proverbs 3:13

"Be not conformed to this world: but be ye transformed by the renewing of your mind." Romans 12:2

"Let this mind be in you, which was also in Christ Jesus." Philippians 2:5

For more information on the Sabbath Day write to *Amazing Facts* at P.O. Box 909, Roseville, CA 95678-0909 or *Amazing Facts Prison Ministry* at P.O. Box 13206, Fort Wayne, IN 46897-6704. Or go to www.amazingfacts.org. Here you can sign up for free Bible studies, and receive information on several topics. May God richly bless you as you study and share the Good News with others!

List of *Amazing Facts* Bible Study Topics:

1. Why you can trust the Bible.
2. The origin of evil.
3. How to obtain Christ's free gift of salvation.
4. **What will heaven be like?**
5. How to have a happy, holy marriage.
6. The Biblical relationship of the Law and grace.
7. God's test of loyalty.
8. **The glorious second coming of Christ.**
9. The meaning and method of baptism.
10. A step-by-step study on the mystery of death.
11. The Biblical description of hell.
12. What happens during the millennium?
13. Bible facts about dieting and health.
14. How God's Law brings freedom.
15. **Who is the Antichrist?**
16. The three angels of *Revelation chapter 14.*
17. What does Jesus do in the heavenly sanctuary?
18. When does judgment begin?
19. Are you ready to face the Judge?
20. **The mark of the beast.**
21. The United States in Bible prophecy.
22. Satan's great deception.
23. The Bible identifies God's End-Time church.
24. What does the Bible say about prophets and visions?
25. God's plan for financial prosperity.
26. Principles for a joyful Christian life.
27. **What is the sin that God cannot forgive?**

—TWENTY-EIGHT—
A Call to Surrender

Jesus Christ, the only Son of God, came not only to offer up Himself as a sacrifice for our sins, but to reveal to us the loving kindness of His Father. Who is also our Creator, Sustainer of life, as well as our Father and Friend. Remember this, my friend, Jesus said:

"All that the Father giveth Me shall come to Me; and him that cometh to Me I will in no wise cast out." John 6:37

"Cast thy burden upon the LORD, and He shall sustain thee." Psalms 55:22

Please give Jesus a chance.

"Trust in the LORD with all thine heart; and lean not unto thine own understanding." Proverbs 3:5

"For [as] the heavens are higher than the earth, so are My ways higher than your ways, and My thoughts than your thoughts." Isaiah 55:9

"In all thy ways acknowledge Him, and He shall direct thy paths." Proverbs 3:6

Please don't be afraid to ask Jesus Christ to come into your heart and help you; and know that the help that He offers may not be what you have in mind, but He knows what is best for you. This is one of the greatest things that I have learned when calling on the name of the Lord. Yes, God is interested in you personally. He is interested in your fears, doubts, sickness, and you daily trials. Maybe it is just trying to make ends meet from a budget that does not provide. He is interested.

When Moses asked God, *"I beseech Thee, show me Thy glory."* God said to him, *"I will make all My goodness pass before thee, and I will announce the name of the Lord before thee." (Exodus 33:18, 19)*

My friend, I would like you to think about something for a moment before we go on. You do realize Moses was a human being just like us. He even killed a man. (See *Exodus 2:12*) He also asked for forgiveness too. He was sorry for his sins. So how about asking God to forgive you and accept Jesus as your Saviour and then ask God to show you His glory

> *"And the LORD passed by before him, and proclaimed, The LORD, The LORD God,* ***merciful and gracious, longsuffering, and abundant in goodness and truth, Keeping mercy for thousands, forgiving iniquity and transgression and sin, and that will by no means clear [the guilty].****" Exodus 34:6, 7*

May you be touched by the goodness of God as you pray for Him to show you His glory. I pray you will hear the voice of God speaking to you in these next verses. These are just some of the many appeals our Father in heaven is making to you and me from His throne.

> *"Look unto Me, and be ye saved, all the ends of the earth: for I am] God, and [there is] none else." Isaiah 45:22*

Do you hear the tender voice of Jesus saying:

> *"Come unto Me, all [ye] that labour and are heavy laden, and I will give you rest." Matthew 11:28*

"Neither is there salvation in any other: for there is none other name under heaven given among men, whereby we must be saved." Acts 4:12

"Come now, and let us reason together, saith the LORD: though your sins be as scarlet, they shall be as white as snow; though they be red like crimson, they shall be as wool." Isaiah 1:18

Here God invites you to talk with Him. He understands how you are feeling and knows what is happening in your heart. It does not matter what you have done or how far in darkness you may have sunk. He longs to wash you clean. Jesus promised:

"If we confess our sins, He is faithful and just to forgive us our] sins, and to cleanse us from all unrighteousness." I John 1:9

What a loving Heavenly Father we have. What wonderful appeals to you and me. Jesus says to us:

"I will never leave thee, nor forsake thee ..." Hebrews 13:5

"Lo, I am with you alway, [even] unto the end of the world." Matthew 28:20

"I will not leave you comfortless: I will come to you." John 14:18

You may think that the Lord has forsaken you because of the trials you may be facing, or because of a certain situation you may be in; but hear the voice of the Lord:

"Can a woman forget her sucking child, that she should not have compassion on the son of her womb?

yea, they may forget, yet will I not forget thee. Behold, I have graven thee upon the palms of [My] hands." Isaiah 49:15, 16

What compassion, what love, what comfort He offers; for Jesus Christ will forever bear the scars upon His hands. How could He forget you, my friend? I pray that you will answer to His calling today and invite Jesus to come into your heart and heal, comfort, restore, and wipe away your tears and fears then fill you with His peace and joy.

"As I live, saith the Lord GOD, I have no pleasure in the death of the wicked; but that the wicked turn from his way and live: turn ye, turn ye from your evil ways; for why will ye die?" Ezekiel 33:11

God offers you eternal life. The gift of salvation is free. Please, don't hesitate another moment, invite Jesus in now; for this is the will of God. My friend, Jesus Christ longs to bring us home; yes, and that means you. It is His will that we be with Him where He is. *(John 17:24)* Soon He will return to take those that have accepted Him as their Saviour, back to His kingdom, Jesus says:

"Let not your heart be troubled: ye believe in God, believe also in Me. In My Father's house are many mansions: if [it were] not [so], I would have told you. I go to prepare a place for you. And if I go and prepare a place for you, I will come again, and receive you unto myself; that where I am, [there] ye may be also." John 14:1–3

God, our Father, is not slack concerning this promise that Jesus Christ has made:

"The Lord is not slack concerning his promise, as some men count slackness; but is longsuffering to us-ward,

> *not willing that any should perish, but that all should come to repentance." II Peter 3:9*

What love, what patience our Father has. He does not want to lose one person. He is longing for all sinners to confess and acknowledge their sin and to call upon Him for forgiveness and cleansing. He calls upon us to be honest with Him as well as with ourselves. And, my friend, He will even help us with this part of our relationship with Him as well. If we would but behold His only Son upon the cross, and ask God to open the eyes of our hearts, we will see that the goodness of God our Father, *"will lead us to repentance." (Romans 2:4)*

> *"If we say that we have no sin, we deceive ourselves, and the truth is not in us. If we confess our sins, He is faithful and just to forgive us [our] sins, and to cleanse us from all unrighteousness." I John 1:8, 9*

> *"For this is the will of God, [even] your sanctification." (That is to make you holy.) I Thessalonians 4:3*

It is God's will to give us good things. (*Matthew 7:11)* Things that will bring us into a closer walk with Him, things that will develop our character to be more like His, and things that will help us be of comfort to others that we may comfort them with the comfort that we ourselves have received.

> *"Every good gift and every perfect gift is from above, and cometh down from the Father of lights, with whom is no variableness, neither shadow of turning." James 1:17*

One of the greatest gifts that our Father longs to give us is the Holy Spirit. Jesus said:

"If ye then, being evil, know how to give good gifts unto your children: how much more shall [your] heavenly Father give the Holy Spirit to them that ask Him?" Luke 11:13

"When He, the Spirit of truth, is come, He will guide you into all truth ... Sanctify them through Thy truth." John 16:13; 17:17

This is the will of God, to have all people saved and to come to the knowledge of the truth. (*I Timothy 2:4)* May we search to know the love of Christ and be filled with all the fullness of God.

"That ye might be filled with all the fulness of God ... we all come in the unity of the faith, and of the knowledge of the Son of God, unto a perfect man, unto the measure of the stature of the fulness of Christ." Ephesians 3:19; 4:13

Let us praise His name for His Word that gives us hope. What an awesome God we have to make such appeals and reveal His will. And, yes, there is so much more He desires to share with you if you would just give Him a chance. You have nothing to lose, and eternal life to gain.

I will pray with you right now before we go on any further: "Oh, Father, we come in the name of Jesus Christ our Saviour, Thy only Son; Whom You gave to die for our sins. Father, please take my heart as I am too weak to give it. It belongs to Thee, Father, for Thy Son has purchased it with His blood. Make it pure and holy for I cannot keep it. Save me, Oh Lord, in spite of my un-Christlike self. Take me in Thy hands, like the potter does with the clay, and shape and mold me into the image Thy would have me to be. Make me like Thy Son and use me to witness to the world, lifting up Jesus that all may be drawn unto Him. Amen."

I would like to share with you a quote from one of my favorite books:

> *"The world's Redeemer accepts men as they are, with all their wants, imperfections, and weaknesses; and He will not only cleanse from sin and grant redemption through His blood, but will satisfy the heart-longing of all who consent to wear His yoke, to bear His burden. It is His purpose to impart peace and rest to all who come to Him for the bread of life. He requires us to perform only those duties that will lead our steps to heights of bliss to which the disobedient can never attain. The true, joyous life of the soul is to have Christ formed within, the hope of glory." Steps to Christ, pg. 46*

I realize that some people think that they need to get all cleaned up before they come to Jesus; but does one take a bath before taking a shower? Invite Jesus, the King of Glory, in now. I will be looking for you in the Kingdom.

—Twenty-nine—

What I Am Doing Now

I am currently working for myself doing construction work. I do outreach and prison ministry using the *Amazing Facts* Bible study guides, and other resources that the Lord leads me to use. Around Christmas time, I dedicate 2 weeks to just traveling and speaking at county jails and witnessing to prisoners through the "Christmas Behind Bars" ministry with my good friend, Lemuel Vega. I travel to wherever I am invited to share my testimony. Sometimes I get invited to come back and do sermons as well. It is my prayer that some day I will be able to attend an Evangelism School, and then to wherever God leads me to be a tool in His hands. I have surrendered my will to Jesus Christ, may He do with me what would be best for the Kingdom of God.

If you would like to make a donation to the author to help support prison ministry and to spread the Gospel truth, you may send check or money order to: Ministry of Truth, P.O. Box 249, Edwardsburg, MI 49112. All donations are tax deductible.

If you would like a copy of any of the poems and reflections you may send $14.99 to the above address. This price includes shipping and handling. All poems will come in an 8x10 frame, with any reflections attached separately.

If you would like the author to speak at your local church or at the end of an evangelistic meeting, you may e-mail him at: ministryoftruth@verizon.net, or call 1-877-778-7884

If you are struggling with drugs, alcohol, nicotine, or an eating disorder please contact Wildwood Hospital, Von Sparrow (Administrator) at 706-820-1493 or Wildwood Health Retreat (Director) Lew and Darline Keith at 931-724-2443 or 931-724-6706. Wildwood Health Retreat Specializing in Life Style Changes.